MODEL MADNESS

ONCE I BUILT A RAILROAD,
MADE IT RUN

BYRON BABBISH

Cover Photograph: The author's son Michael is a bit upset about his derailed model train in the background.

Copyright © 2014 Byron Babbish

No portion of this book may be reproduced by any process or means without the written permission of the publisher.

Published by Aboard & Abroad Productions LLC

www.aboardandabroad.com

2616 Kopson Court, Bloomfield Hills, MI 48304

Printed by CreateSpace, an Amazon.com company.

ISBN: 1494970007

ISBN-13: 978- 1494970000

DEDICATION

This book is dedicated to the late William R. Dewey, Jr. and the late Ned Finkbeiner, the two people who infected me with Model Train Madness.

CONTENTS

    ACKNOWLEDGMENTS   i

1. LIONEL TRAINS AND OTHER EARLY MODEL RAILROAD ADVENTURES   1

2. INTRODUCTION TO HO SCALE AT MY NEIGHBOR'S MODEL RAILROAD: THE KISHACOQUILLAS VALLEY   9

3. THE ERIE & MICHIGAN RAILWAY AND NAVIGATION COMPANY MODEL RAILROAD   14

4. MY FIRST MODEL RAILROAD: MANISTIQUE & LAKE SUPERIOR RAILROAD   26

5. BULDING A MODEL RAILROAD FOR MY CHILDREN AND THE EXPANSION OF MINE   97

6. MODELING THE ANN ARBOR RAILROAD   127

7. MODELING THE GREEN BAY & WESTERN RAILROAD   144

8. MODELING GRAND TRUNK WESTERN AND CANADIAN NATIONAL RAILROADS   157

ACKNOWLEDGMENTS

In addition to the late Ned Finkbeiner and the late Bill Dewey, to whom this book is dedicated, I want to acknowledge my wife, Elaine, who always encouraged my Model Train Madness, and also the group of model railroaders I have associated with over the last 35 years who kept the hobby interesting and active for me.

Introduction

As will be seen in this book, model railroading has been a great adventure for me. It has been a life-long madness I have had, starting when I was very young. It has taught me a lot: history and geography, carpentry and electrical skills. It has made me many friends and has resulted in literally building a railroad, albeit a model railroad, and making it run, something not many people can say they have done. As you will see, I have Model Train Madness.

This book is my attempt to describe and explain my Model Train Madness: from the days of the Lionel trains at Christmas, to being a visitor at others' model railroads, to the construction of my own model railroad and then to the evolution of my layout into other model railroads over the years. My Model Train Madness was greatly infected by my interest in the real railroads. Surprisingly, model railroading turned out to be great preparation for me working on a real railroad, which is the story for another Madness book someday.

One aspect of my model railroading adventures that this book is intended to convey is that a model railroad doesn't have to be a static display or one that merely has trains running in circles. It doesn't have to be a piece of art (though I think of mine as such) but, instead, a living and evolving adventure that is constantly changing over time and that is used as a medium to better understand how the real railroads worked and how they fit into our society. History and operations are the two greatest things I have obtained from my model railroads. As you will see, my model railroad evolved into different model railroads over time as I wanted to expand my layout and pursue the adventure of modeling a different railroad without totally abandoning all the work I had done up to that point.

As second aspect of Model Train Madness that I want to convey is the friendships that comes out of the hobby. It is an activity that involves many people: from the initial idea to build a model railroad, what it should be modeled on, how to build it, how to operate it, how to fix it and, most importantly, having a bunch of friends with Model Train Madness at your house making your model railroad run like the real thing.

CHAPTER 1

LIONEL TRAINS AND OTHER EARLY MODEL RAILROAD ADVENTURES

Almost everyone my age (born 1953) had a toy train as a kid. Most of us had a Lionel "0-27" gauge train set we received as a Christmas present one year. I had a very nice Lionel train set. I had it all set up on a large piece of plywood, first in my first childhood home in Detroit and then, later, in my suburban home in Birmingham, Michigan.

Though, like most kids, my interest in my Lionel trains peaked and ebbed over the years, it was always there in the basement ready to play with. I had three distinct Lionel train sets. The first was a 1957-era one with a Milwaukee Road F-7 A-B locomotive set, freight cars, caboose and some industries and buildings that worked in conjunction with some of the freight cars. The second train set was a passenger train with a steam locomotive and four passenger cars, two being domed cars and one a round-end observation car. The third was Lionel's 1800's-era "General" steam engine passenger train.

In addition, I had some extra freight cars as well as a Rio Grande industrial switcher that had a snowplow on it. I also had a powered trolley and a track inspection car. I had plenty of track, two manual-throw turnouts and some buildings.

I spent a lot of time playing with my Lionel railroad until

I was ten or eleven years old. When we moved to our new house in the suburbs in 1960, we brought the train table with us but I never tacked down the track to the plywood. I was glad I didn't as I always had a lot of fun designing new and different track layouts and not being locked into the same one. This was a prelude for things to come.

I do not recall ever doing much more than running trains around the track, usually very fast, which was typical Lionel. I recall having fun with the switches but not for switching cars but, instead, routing the trains onto another route that would be longer or shorter than the first. I never really knew the significance of the types of locomotives or freight cars I had other than passenger cars were one type of train and freight cars the other type.

I remember going with my dad once on a trip to a store that was somehow related to my Lionel trains. It was some where in Detroit. I don't remember any trains on display or anything to make it seem like it was a model railroad store. I seem to recall that the place was called "The Train Doctor," so it was probably a model railroad repair shop instead of a store selling trains. I just remember a man standing behind a counter that was carved out of the wall. Years later I remember dad pointing out some building in Ferndale, Michigan and telling me that the Train Doctor was there now.

My best friend Jerry also had a model train set. He had one made by American Flyer and I will always remember the Santa Fe passenger train with a set of silver and red locomotives he had. Jerry and I always would argue as to what was better, Lionel or American Flyer? These debates would always end with Jerry pointing out that no one could take any real railroad seriously that ran on three-rail tracks instead of the prototypical two-rail tracks. I never had a comeback to that.

Of course, he was referring to the three-rail tracks that Lionel always used with the center rail supplying the electrical current to power the electric locomotive. I never understood this either but, except for this little quirk, was still convinced that Lionel was better. Well, Lionel did survived American Flyer.

My favorite Lionel trains were the military ones that Lionel bought out in the early 1960's. This was in response to the Cold War with the Soviet Union and the military buildup going on at this time. I had a couple of rocket launching cars, a helicopter and satellite launching car, a target balloon car and, my favorite, a target boxcar that exploded when hit. This brought playing with trains to a new level that, in retrospect, was an introduction to "operating" trains instead of just "playing" with them as you had to set off the target car on a siding then position the train so the rocket launcher was in the right spot to shoot at it. More on "operating" model trains later.

The worst thing to ever happen to Lionel trains was the TV series *"The Adams Family."* You know what show I am referring to. In this comedy TV series that was extremely popular in the 1960's, the father, Gomez Adams, loved to play with his Lionel trains in the basement. The only problem was that his idea of fun was to have these tremendous train wrecks with them, all fitting in with the bizarre behavior of the Adams Family.

Before Gomez I do not think that I ever thought of playing with my trains this way. After Gomez this was the only way to play with them. I guess the good point was that it got me back into the basement to play with trains. The bad point was that I did a lot of damage to my trains by having these wrecks, a fact that I regret to this day.

At some point, the Lionel trains were all put away in boxes and stored. Luckily I had the sense to save them when my parents moved out of the old house and took them with me. It was 1984 and I had my own house so I just took the boxes and stored them in my attic. I did wrap and pack them up quite well, each car and locomotive individually wrapped in newspaper.

It was the Christmas of 1986 that I had the idea to take out my Lionel trains and put them around the Christmas tree. My first child was born in 1985 so it was probably because of her that I thought of it. I was amazed that they still worked pretty well and were in fairly good shape. We had neighbors over that Christmas and they all had young children. I remember turning on the train and, for the rest of the evening, the children just laid there on the carpet, their heads on their hands propped up by their elbows laying alongside the track, watching the train go round and round the tree. It was like they were hypnotized. It was really amazing what an affect Lionel trains had on these children.

Well, needless to say, putting the old Lionel trains under the tree became a Christmas tradition after that. Soon I had three kids and we did this every Christmas since then. It had become an important part of our Christmas decorating and celebrating when the kids were young.

When the kids were a bit older they became bored with just watching the train run in circles. A game they came up with was to use the freight cars, mostly flat cars or gondolas, to transport small toys or other small things from one side of the Christmas tree to the other where another kid would remove it and send something else back. It was always a big surprise to the receiving kid what they would receive from the other. For years the kids played this game with the Lionel trains. Quickly the "loads" became Christmas decoration taken from off the tree. As they got older the oldest child was allowed to be engineer and run the train for the others so I did not have to supervise their play. One time I came by and the entire bottom third of the Christmas Tree was undecorated and laying in piles by the kids' location on either side of the tree for loading and unloading on the train. Boy, were they having fun.

After a few years I noticed that these Christmas Lionel operating sessions were taking a toll on my 1950-era trains. Plus, the kids were getting older and more responsible. I looked back and saw that I was about their age when I received my Lionel trains. It became clear that, even though they liked playing with mine, if I didn't buy them their own trains now they wouldn't have their childhood Lionel trains to pull out at Christmas and play with their kids.

So, for a number of Christmases, I would buy my children Lionel trains as gifts. They all received a locomotive at one time or other and one or two freight cars often appeared as Christmas gifts. My son Michael, the one who expressed the most interest in model trains, even got a complete Lionel trainset one Christmas. After a few years they didn't express an interest in receiving these as gifts so I stopped. But at least they all have enough Lionel Trains of their own to put together a train someday for their children at Christmas.

My kids' favorite Lionel cars of my era were the cold war military cars too, just like me. By luck, Lionel reissued some of these when I was buying toy trains as gifts for them and I purchased a number of these for them, giving mine a break.

Now the kids are adults and on their own and so this tradition has stopped. I will admit that I always liked Lionel and what it represents in model railroading: a fun, non-serious, just run-those-trains-fast hobby and enjoy watching them go round and round. I guess it is the little boy in me still that is attracted to Lionel trains.

There were two other model railroad events that I recall as a child. One was discovering by accident a model railroad club that had an "O" gauge layout at the Michigan State Fair Grounds in Detroit. It was located below the grandstands of the outdoor sports arena. Right outside of it was a huge steam locomotive that was on display there. It was 1959 and we were visiting the State Fair and stumbled upon the steam locomotive on display. We almost missed the fact that the model railroad club was right there and had an open house during the State Fair. I remember going inside the door and into a small waiting room with the far wall being a large window. You would stand at the window and see all the model trains racing around the layout, dozens at a time. You could also smell that ozone aroma of those transformers powering those trains from in the train room.

A second model railroad event happened a few years later after we moved to the suburbs. Grand Trunk Western Railroad went through the town of Birmingham that we lived in and had a nice depot there. The attic of the depot was rented to a model railroad club. Each Christmas they had an open house and my dad took me there one time. It was HO guage and I vaguely remember that the layout was modeled after the Grand Trunk Western line. I recognized names of local towns like Royal Oak, Ferndale, Clarkston, Fenton and Holly that were painted on locations along the model railroad. Trains were running on the layout but I think the fact that they were so small compared to the Lionel-sized trains I had didn't lend itself to interest me that much. Even though I didn't realize it at the time, it was my first introduction to modeling a model railroad after a real railroad line. This was an important concept later in my life that greatly affected my Model Train Madness.

Below is my daughter Brigid enjoying a model toy train the kids received one Christmas. She worked on a real railroad for a month during her senior year of high school as part of Senior Career Project. I am sure this had a lot to do with that.

CHAPTER 2

INTRODUCTION TO HO SCALE AT MY NEIGHBOR'S MODEL RAILROAD: THE KISHACOQUILLAS VALLEY

A family moved into my neighborhood when I was a teenager whose father had a profound influence on my life and probably was the one that really infected me with Model Train Madness. The family was from Pennsylvania. The two boys were younger than I was so I didn't really play much with them. But I sure played a lot with their father, Ned, as he had a model railroad!

Ned was the greatest model railroader. He modeled in HO scale. Though he didn't have a model railroad layout in his house at first, he did have boxes and boxes stored in the basement containing tons of model railroad locomotives and freight cars. I also found out that he liked real railroads and that he knew a whole lot about them.

I cannot exactly recall when all this happened and maybe it slowly happened over time but as a result of this neighbor I became in love (again) with railroads, both real and model railroads.

I was aware of HO scale model railroads. I even had a small HO train set at one time but it seemed so toy-like compared to my O-27 gauge Lionel set that I never really had any interest in it.

What really caught my attention about Ned's model trains were all the brass steam locomotives he had. They were all so beautiful and detailed, like little mechanical gems. I remember first seeing brass HO locomotives at a hobby shop located in Ferndale, Michigan. I used to talk my father into taking me there and would wonder all around it, fascinated by everything in the store, especially the model trains. The brass steam locomotives were in a glass showcase located right when you came into the store and you couldn't miss them.

I had never known that each railroad's steam locomotives were usually unique to that railroad. I found this out through Ned explaining it while showing me his brass models. You could really notice the differences when seeing a HO scale locomotive.

At some point in time Ned started building a small model railroad in his basement. I remember helping him out at times. I worked with him on the benchwork and planning of the track layout. I helped him do the electrical wiring. It was a lot of fun and a great experience. The year was 1974. Ned's model railroad was named The Kishacoquillas Valley Railroad and it was based on a real railroad in Pennsylvania. This was now the second time I saw a model railroad modeled after a real railroad. Ned's model railroad was my introduction to the joys of model railroading and, in particular, the benefits of modeling with HO scale model trains.

At some point Ned had his model railroad built enough so that we could run some trains back and forth on it. This was a lot of fun. Once, as payment for collecting their mail and watching their house when they were on vacation, Ned purchased for me my first HO model diesel locomotive. It was an Athearn EMD SW-7 switcher. He even painted it up in a Grand Trunk Western Railroad paint scheme, as he knew that was my favorite railroad, and customized it by adding handrails and directional lighting. I would leave it at his layout and operate it whenever I came over.

Ned not only introduced me to model railroading but also to running model railroads like the real railroads operate. We called this "operating" the model railroad instead of just "playing" with it. Being a Lionel model railroader, I thought that model railroads only ran in circles and very fast. Ned's layout was a "point to point" layout so no circular running was available. What Ned did was make trains where each freight car in a train had a destination on the railroad, either an industry that it was to be delivered to or another railroad that it was being interchanged with. This opened up a whole new aspect of the hobby to me and, to this day, the "operations" of a model railroad is the most important part of the hobby to me.

Ned also taught me how one can model a railroad either based on a real railroad during a certain historical time period or a based on a fictional railroad during a historical time period. This introduced the historical aspect of modeling a railroad to make it have a context and connection with the real thing. Suddenly you have to be concerned about what type of freight cars and locomotives you had on your railroad and even the paint scheme on them so as to match the prototype railroad of that era. Same with the industries on the railroad: They had to be similar to the type of industries that would exist on that railroad in that geographic location in that era. This operational and prototypical aspect of model railroading really added to the intellectual and historical aspect of model railroading far beyond what most people think of the hobby. This is what really attracted me to model railroading and I have Ned to thank for it.

I remember very often ringing Ned's doorbell and asking if I could come and play with the model railroad. It didn't matter if Ned couldn't join me or if Ned was even home at the time as I was always let in. I used to just run trains by myself for an hour or so in his basement, usually using my locomotive. Below is Ned operating at my layout.

At some point in the late 1980's Ned expanded his layout and had a nice operation. It was never much more than tracks on benchwork but he would have regularly scheduled operating sessions and invite people over. We had a lot of fun running trains.

I never understood why Ned never finished bulding his railroad. At some point he became too ill to do so. He had always been a real model railroad fanatic. He purchased tons of locomotives and rolling stock but they all just got stored in boxes, many never to be used. I think Ned kept thinking that he would move back to Pennsylvania when he retired and was waiting to build the model railroad of his dreams then. I kept telling him that he should turn his basement into a hobby shop and sell all his stuff. One year Ned did decide to sell a lot of his brass locomotives, all of which sold at a very good price as brass was probably ten times higher in price than what he paid for them years prior, as he realized he would never use them.

Ned was the man I and everyone went to for model railroading advice and information. He introduced many people to model railroading. He helped many people with their model railroads and with any issues that came up with them. He was also our social director, keeping our circle of model railroaders together and in touch with each other. Ned passed away on May 14, 2009. I certainly miss Ned and am grateful for having known him and for what he taught me about model railroads. I am sure he is operating that railroad he always dreamed of building up there in heaven.

CHAPTER 3

THE ERIE & MICHIGAN RAILWAY AND NAVIGATION COMPANY MODEL RAILROAD

In the summer of 1976, my neighbor Ned invited me to join him operating a model railroad at a friend's house in Birmingham, Michigan, my hometown. Ned had been there the month before and couldn't stop talking about it. I was twenty-two years old at the time.

The model railroad was located in the basement of a gentleman named Bill. Part of Bill's basement was an office and it had its own entrance off the driveway of the house. I remember having to park on the street as there were a lot of cars there already that summer evening. Before we let ourselves inside, Ned turned to me and said, "Byron, from now on no more of this 'Mr.' stuff. Just call me Ned." Wow, I had arrived.

And boy, had I arrived. I remember entering the train room and being amazed. For the first time in my life I saw a large, completed HO Scale model railroad. It was beautiful. Not only was the size of it awesome (it went around the entire basement twice with a large island in the middle), but the number of freight cars, the buildings and the scenery made it look like a work of art. And the really amazing thing is that it just wasn't a static piece of art but, instead, a working model railroad as I was to find out that evening.

Bill had picked the year 1933 to model as it was his

railroad era. Because of this all the locomotives were brass steam engines. Bill decided to model a railroad named the Erie & Michigan Railway and Navigation Company. Its route was from Toledo, Ohio running diagonally across the State of Michigan to the City of Manistee on Lake Michigan. The E&M, as it was known, was the name of a very short Michigan Railroad located in Alabaster, just south of Tawas City on Lake Huron. Bill's E&M was nothing like the real one. It was better.

Steam was king on the E&M and, when I first visited the layout, the steam locomotives were in the form of smaller locomotives, very typical of a small, marginal railroad of this era. Bill was inspired by the George Hilton book on the Maryland & Pennsylvania Railroad and his operations and motive power mirrored that of the Ma & Pa. His geographical location, however, mirrored that of the Ann Arbor Railroad. As a matter of fact, the Ann Arbor RR was a fictional competitor of the E&M and interchanged with it at Cadillac on the layout.

This model railroad also ran like a real railroad, so not only did it have the realistic looks, it had realistic operations. This is what I fell in love with about the E&M and model railroading.

Bill even had a dispatcher controlling the trains operating on the railroad. He located the dispatcher's "office" in another area of the basement so the dispatcher couldn't see what was going on in the train room. He could only "see" the railroad by his dispatcher's board and by verbal communication with crews and tower operators.

This concept of a dispatcher on a model railroad was really something to me. When I first saw that dispatcher's board I said that I never wanted that job as it looked very difficult and confusing. The dispatcher was responsible to give permission to every train to proceed from point A to point B. Often there were three or four trains on the railroad running at the same time. Bill also had passenger trains running on a time schedule and they had priority over all other trains. The dispatcher had to arrange meets in towns on sidings to allow one train to pass another as the entire mainline was but a single track. Often there was a local train and locomotive in a town that had to clear the siding and mainline so the dispatcher could have a meet of two mainline freight trains or with a passenger train in town.

Bill also had a clock that was the official time of the model railroad and all operations were based on this time, especially the passenger trains that had to follow their schedules. The clock ran fast so that one minute real time was six minutes railroad time. This allowed for a twelve-hour railroad day to occur in two real hours, the usual length of time for an operating session.

After that first visit to Bill's railroad, I was definitely bitten by the model railroad bug. I was invited back month after month. I tried to make every session and did so for almost 20 years.

All new crew members on the E&M started off as crews on the passenger trains. This was an easier job as you didn't have to know how his card system for freight worked and you usually just followed the tracks from one end to the other, stopping at the train stations along the way, hopefully in a timely manner. This way you learned the most important part of the model railroad, the geography of the layout: where the towns were and what their names were. You also found out where the trains were headed to at any point on the line and which way they were headed and how to describe it to the dispatcher.

The hardest part of learning an operating railroad like Bill's was learning the operational aspect of it. Trains were not just running in circles on this kind of railroad. They were going places and then the tracks stop and they must come back. Once you got the passenger trains down, Bill would promote you to a through-freight train. This involved some understanding of the card system used on the railroad for the freight cars. Usually the through-freight trains just went from one end to the other, similar to a passenger train, with little or no switching in between.

On Bill's layout each freight car had a card in form of a library pocket card. Typed on the card was the type of freight car it was (boxcar, gondola, etc.), the owner, the initials and number, and a short description of what the car looked like based on its color and logo. Also typed on the card was the destination on the railroad to return the car to when it was empty.

Into the pocket card went a color-coded index card that

was the waybill. All boxcar waybills had an orange index card, for example. The waybill index card indicated where the freight car was being delivered to and what it contained. The delivery location was usually an industry in a city on the railroad and it gave the name of the industry and the city. Like on a real railroad, all freight cars on the model railroad are headed somewhere on the railroad, either to an industry to unload or load it or to a connecting railroad to get it off the railroad.

When the freight car was delivered to its location, as indicated on the waybill, the index card waybill instructed you to either remove it or turn it over. When removed, the next destination for the freight car was the one typed on the library pocket card at the top. This was because the car was now considered empty of its freight loading and was to return to its home railroad. Sometimes the waybill instructed you to turn it over and reinsert it. It then gave the car a new destination; the theory being that it was an empty car delivered to that industry for loading and now that it was loaded it was to go to another industry to deliver its load.

When it was an empty car returning home and the car arrived at its connecting railroad it would be given a new waybill with a new location on the E&M and thus become a loaded freight car for delivery. This card system was basically "perpetual" as a freight car always had a place to be delivered to.

Another aspect of the operational aspects of Bill's model railroad was that he would have hidden tracks, usually at connecting railroads, where freight cars would be delivered to and remain at for a long time before coming out again onto the railroad. This was called a "staging area" and allowed a fresh influx of cars every session that have not been seen sometimes for months. It also allowed getting more freight cars on the railroad and more variety. Usually there would be two or three hidden tracks and the last one filled up would wait until the other ones where pulled first: a first-in last-out method. Connecting railroads also gave some variety to the model railroad as it allowed locomotives of other railroads to appear on the model railroad for interchange of freight cars, just like the real ones. All railroads connect with other railroads. This is known as interstate commerce.

Well, I worked my way up the seniority roster at Bill's model railroad. One job no one really wanted as it was not really running trains was the dispatcher's job. One day, after a couple years of operating on his layout, Bill asked me to be dispatcher. I had never worked so hard in my life. You had to be scale hours ahead of everything to plan out each move. You had to anticipate passenger trains and know their schedules, know where every train was, and, a lesson not quickly learned, expect whatever could go wrong to go wrong and work that into your planning. Boy, did I have a great time as dispatcher. For many years that was all I ever wanted to be at Bill's session, the dispatcher.

The train crews and yardmasters communicated with the dispatcher by a closed-circuit telephone system. On the walls at each town was a telephone with an open line to the dispatcher. In 1933 there was no radio communication between crews and dispatchers as there is now. Back then it was all telegraph and telephones from the station agents located in each town and the yardmasters' offices. Technically the crew didn't talk to the dispatcher but the station agent did as the train arrived or passed through his town. This way the dispatcher knew where the trains were or had a pretty good idea. On the E&M the train crews acted as the station agents and called the dispatcher themselves when they arrived at a town.

The dispatcher had control of all the switches on the mainline on the whole railroad. This way he could route trains safely to get them to their location and to set up meets with other trains in towns, all under his command. Each of these switches on Bill's layout were electric switches and had a toggle on the dispatcher's board on the diagram where it was located on the railroad. The dispatcher could give "local control" of a switch to a crew and they could operate the switch from a control panel located in each town. This was so local trains could be given permission to occupy the entire town and throw all their own switches as needed to switch the town's industries until the dispatcher took this privilege away from them in order to route a through-train through town. As you can see, a dispatcher not only needed to know the railroad and all the sidings but also how the operations went. Of course, the passenger trains and their schedules were the dispatcher's first priority, and the biggest headache.

In the early years of Bill's operating sessions, we used to have a break halfway through a session and we all changed jobs for the second half of the sessions. This was also true of the dispatcher's job. We also would keep track of the number of freight cars (not trains) that went across the railroad on any given night. This led to some competition to see who could move the most cars and we always tried to beat the record. Ron and I as dispatchers (he for one-half of a session and I for the other half) hold the record set in 1988 of moving 496 freight cars in one session. That was a lot of trains considering the train length was 10 cars maximum on Bill's railroad.

After you got the hang of the card system you would be assigned a local train. A local train went from a freight yard to a town with a train full of cars to be delivered to the local industries in that town. Now you needed to know how to operate a train over the line and communicate with the dispatcher by telephone, where the towns were, how the card system worked, how to physically switch cars out of the train to the proper place, the location of the industries and, on top of this, removing empty freight cars from the industries as appropriate to take back to the freight yard when done. It was a rare event when you were a local in a town and didn't have your work interrupted at least once while you were there by the dispatcher making sure you were cleared of the mainline or siding or both for a through-train or a meet of trains in that town, just like on the real railroads. Even though the local crew had local control of all the switches in that town, they had to keep the mainline clear at all times unless they had permission to occupy it by the dispatcher.

The "high seniority" operators on the E&M usually were the ones who were in charge of the two large freight yards. These were the yardmasters. Their job was to organize freight cars in their yards into departing trains and sending these trains out of the yards to their destinations with a road crew. This involved accepting arriving trains and classifying the cars as to their next destination. Thus, the yardmaster had to know the railroad inside and out as every train leaving the yard had to be correct for where it was going.

I had many years of fun operating Bill's model railroad. At some point in the 1980's his brass steam locomotives were wearing out. Bill decided to replace them with diesels, which were coming out in HO Scale in high-quality, inexpensive plastic models at the time. He moved the date of his model railroad's era to 1959, which also required updating a lot of his rolling stock. This was a pretty exciting change though I will always miss the 1933 steam-era E&M.

At about the time of this updating program Bill also converted to "Dynatrol" carrier control. At first this worked great but electrical and manufacturer problems loomed in the near future with it. Bill also expanded his layout into his basement office by creating a large boat yard in Filler City, the western end of the railroad, and building a large area that was Milwaukee, Wisconsin. To get from Filler City to Milwaukee he had a friend build a scale model of a Lake Michigan carferry that was on a table that had rollers so it could "sale" across Lake Michigan with a carload full of freight cars between these two port towns.

The addition of Milwaukee and the carferry was really something. It was a very unique aspect of model railroading that modeled a unique aspect of Michigan railroading. Before this the "carferry" was just a hidden storage track that was switched.

Within a few years of building the Milwaukee extension, Bill decided to retire and move out of his house to a condo. He had to dismantle the E&M. Bill had a "last run" one day where all his friends were invited then he dismantled it. It was a sad day for me personally as the E&M was a major influence on me and my Model Train Madness.

The only good thing about this was that I had begun model railroading myself by this time and was able to purchase from Bill a lot of rolling stock and buildings to put on my layout.

A number of years later, Bill decided to build another model railroad in the basement of his condo. He reverted back to the 1930's with it and built a magnificent layout based on the Pere Marquette Railroad. It was an all-steam locomotive layout like his original E&M layout was but this time it was big-time steam running on a very long model railroad. Bill died a few years after completing this new model railroad and we all miss him greatly and are the better off because of him and his model railroads.

CHAPTER 4

MY FIRST MODEL RAILROAD: MANISTIQUE & LAKE SUPERIOR RAILROAD

Ever since my model railroad experiences with Ned and Bill starting in the mid-1970's, I had always wanted to build my own model railroad. When first married, I lived in a flat that had a basement that we shared with another family so a model railroad there was out of the question. When we bought our first house in 1983, it did not have a basement and nowhere else to build a model railroad. I remember a basement being a criteria of any house I would consider and the one we eventually bought mistakenly showed on its listing description that it had a basement, otherwise I would probably not have ever looked at it. When we viewed the house we fell in love with it, so much so that my disappointment at discovering that it did not have a basement did not prevent our purchasing it.

Back then we did not have children and I was still very much into watching and photographing real railroads as a hobby. So starting a model railroad was not all that high on my priority list. I did occasionally purchase some freight cars and once let Ned talk me into buying two brass steam locomotive switchers. But other than that, nothing serious.

I always thought that I would build a model railroad based on the real Grand Trunk Western Railroad, as that was my home-town railroad and my favorite. If I did any model railroad thinking or purchasing during these early years it was with GTW in mind.

My first model railroad purchase was sometime in the early 1980's. A local train hobby shop opened in my hometown and I visited it occasionally. For no reason in particular I one day purchased five HO scale freight cars. They were Train Miniature brand and were on sale. Three were X-29 type steel 40-foot boxcars (one each for Lehigh New England Railroad, Pennsylvania Railroad and Central Railroad of New Jersey), one was a doublesheathed wooden boxcar in the Rutland Railroad yellow and green scheme and one was a white and black Lackawanna reefer. That was a big event that I still remember. The cars were on sale for something like $2 each.

Also around this time Ned gave me a wooden model railroad car kit to build. It was a Central Valley side-door caboose. I remember building it very carefully and painting it red and black but leaving it unlettered. As a result of my experience doing this I purchased and built two more such Central Valley brand kits, both for 36-foot boxcars, one for Michigan Central Railroad and the other for Canada Southern Railway. I still own two of these original seven boxcars and the Central Valley caboose, all of which run on my current model railroad. I sold the two Central Valley boxcars to a friend and he ran them on his model railroad as they fit in his 1920's era.

When I moved into my current house in March 1989, I immediately decided to start planning and building a model railroad. I knew my limitations: I had no carpentry, electrical, artistic or modeling skills and I didn't have much money to spend. I had a young family and did find it harder to find the time to go off trainwatching like I used to but did have a lot of time at home when the kids were sleeping or otherwise where I would have time to go downstairs in the basement and work on a model railroad. It was time to start model railroading.

I knew that the first thing I had to decide was what railroad to model. I liked the idea of modeling a fictitious railroad like Bill's E&M. However, I was more intrigued with trying to model a real prototype railroad. I did know that I wanted to model the 1950's era as I wanted to use early diesel locomotives and steam locomotives. I also knew I wanted to have the model railroad set in Michigan somewhere. I also wanted to model a shortline railroad so I could model the whole line in a small amount of space.

So what railroad to model? I had a good-sized basement that my wife let me have one full room of. I wanted to start small, though, and, after visiting so many operating layouts that were never finished, I made a vow that I would totally complete whatever railroad I started before I expanded it or changed it.

I joined a number of railroad historical societies around this time. Some were because I was interested in them for railfanning. Others were because I wanted to know more about their historical real railroad for modeling purposes. The first such historical society I joined was the Ann Arbor Railroad Technical & Historical Association. They covered the prototype railroad real well and did a great job discussing modeling the Ann Arbor Railroad in their quarterly newsletter. They even produced decals for Ann Arbor Railroad HO Scale freight cars and locomotives.

Another early model railroad purchase I had made was a three-pack of Model Die Casting covered hoppers painted up for the Ann Arbor Railroad by a local modeling group.

Little did I know that this was going to be an important purchase for me.

I had a lot of fun deciding what railroad to model. I wrote a number of letters to the editor of the Ann Arbor Technical & Historical Association's newsletter, discussing my decision-making process. I think it would be valuable to attach these letters here instead of trying to capture my thoughts and emotions of that time by writing them anew. As you will see, I sort of fell into my decision of what railroad to model by accident. The letters also detail out the progression of my model railroad building from its humble beginnings to what eventually became its current form.

November 29, 1989

Dear Editor,

Thanks for the complimentary 1990 AARRTHA Calendar and for using one of my shots in it. It is always an honor to have a photo published in the calendar.

I also received your Fall Newsletter the other day and it was the best ever. Not only was the new format super but also so were all the news items in it. I am always interested in reading about the various shortlines in the state and this issue covered so many of them while keeping the Ann Arbor RR connection to them evident.

By far the best article you have ever published, though, was Part I of the Manistique & Lake Superior Railroad story. The M&LS always caught my fancy though I knew so little about it. This article was so well researched and written that it really should be put together in a book. I always thought that the M&LS would be a fun railroad to model, as it was short and uncomplicated and lended itself to a first-time modeler like myself (e.g., a shortline with an easy paint scheme on the locomotive) and I think that this article has made up my mind to model the M&LS.

Could you please send me the address of the author? I would like to inquire about obtaining a copy of the entire manuscript from him so I could begin modeling the M&LS accurately this winter (as you can tell, I cannot wait for all the future issues of *The Double A* newsletter to read the whole story).

What follows is a letter I sent to Hugh Hornstein, the author of the M&LS manuscript referred to in the above letter.

November 30, 1989

Dear Hugh,

I read with great interest Chapter I of *A Brief History of the Manistique & Lake Superior Railroad* that appeared in the Fall, 1989 issue of *The Double A*. I have always been interested in Michigan railroads, especially the shortlines and, in particularly, Michigan's Upper Peninsula shortlines, so you can understand the reasons for my excitement in reading your work.

I have been toying with the idea of model railroading and I thought M&LS would be a good railroad to model as it was short yet interesting, particularly due to its carferry operations. I think your article has pushed me off the fence, especially since it appears that I will know almost everything there is to know about the M&LS after reading the entire manuscript.

Which leads me to the reason for my letter. I would be interested in obtaining a complete copy of your manuscript on the history of the M&LS, as it appears that it may take *The Double A* newsletter years to reproduce it in its entirety. If you have it in a printed form ready for sale please let me know the price and I will send you a check. If instead you would have to run a photocopy of the manuscript and would be willing to do so I would be more than happy to reimburse your photocopying costs involved.

I would also like to encourage you to continue your research and writing on Michigan railroads and to be kept posted when you have manuscripts or books available for sale.

The following letters reproduced below are all "up-date" letters to the editor of the AAT&H Association newsletter describing my thoughts and, later, my decisions on modeling and my progress in modeling.

January 2, 1990

Dear Editor,

I wrote and received a response from Hugh on his M&LS article. He said he would send me a copy of the manuscript soon. He wrote a long letter and sent a number of maps and seemed very nice. I have committed to modeling the M&LS. I am planning on keeping it small and simple (one of the reasons for picking M&LS) and hope that it will dovetail into my modeling a larger Upper Peninsula railroad someday when I decide to go crazy and do a large layout. With the M&LS I keep the Ann Arbor Railroad nexus.

I have been pouring over past issues of *The Double A*

newsletter to find out information about M&LS and also details of the Ann Arbor Railroad as the Annie was its owner railroad and major interchange partner. I always enjoyed the news information in the newsletters and now also enjoy the historical and modeling information. Hugh said in his letter that the AAT&HA has M&LS decals available but I could not find that out from looking in past issues. Could you please send me a list of decals AAT&HA has available? Enclosed is a SASE for that purpose.

I will keep you informed about how modeling the M&LS is going. I do not plan on being too accurate. For instance, I am using an Atlas Alco S-2 as its diesel locomotive instead of an S-3 like the real railroad had and may also run two 0-6-0 switchers at the same time, though I doubt M&LS ran steam and diesel together and, even if they did, it probably was not 0-6-0's as the last issue of *The Double A* showed a Consolidation type. I know, it is guys like me that probably drive guys like you crazy, but I would probably drive myself crazy trying to model it accurately. Matter of fact, I probably would not even get started if that were the case.

But it should be fun and I am very excited about it.

January 22, 1990

Dear Editor,

Thanks for your letter and the decals and decal information. After writing this letter I am sending in my check for the AA-5 decal set. Some day I will do up a modern M&LS boxcar with the set of decals you sent along and either invite you by or send you a picture of it.

I am going to try modeling the M&LS around 1953; the

year they acquired their Alco S-3 diesel locomotive. As I mentioned, I may throw in a steam locomotive or two and my "excuse" will be that it is the year they just dieselized and they were having a good year and needed the steamers for just a little longer. I am interested in reading the rest of the M&LS manuscript of Hugh's to see if this really did occur; though I doubt it did. Also, I would need more locomotives to keep at least a few guys busy at operating sessions.

I really appreciate your bits and pieces of modeling advice on the M&LS. I have been creating a hot item list and, from your letter, I know the Overland Snowplow (OMI #3030) and MDC ore cars are at the top of the list. Though I know they are not perfect, I have picked up seven of the Bev-Bel AA boxcars (two with the solid white pennant and five with the outline pennant) as well as a Wabash boxcar and am planning on doing some AA hoppers. I did buy three of the AA covered hoppers that one of the local railroad historical societies sold a few years back and could always say there was a sand pit up there somewhere for routing them to. I am also on the lookout for old Soo Line and DSS&A freight cars. I heard someone brought out an Athearn boxcar painted for DSS&A a few years back that is apparently out of production and I will probably start hitting some of the flea markets looking for this as well as the other items mentioned above. I saw some kits from a guy named Dennis Storzek from Indiana the other day of three different DSS&A boxcars but they were a little expensive for my budget and probably too complicated for my skills. Anyway, if you ever hear of any of the above for sale by anyone, let me know.

At the risk of boring you further, what I envision is a U-shaped layout, about 12-foot by 8-foot by 12-foot with one 12-foot wall being the City of Manistique. In Manistique there would be the yard, the roundhouse and turntable, four or five industries, the Soo Line interchange and, of course, the carferry. For the time being the carferry would probably be merely a storage track though someday an actual ferry would be nice as well as possibly Ann Arbor's Elberta boat yard somewhere else in the basement (very distant future). The rest of the trackage would merely be a single track mainline with a siding at Hiawatha, Stueben, an interchange with DSS&A, a siding at Shingleton and an extension of the track to the LS&I interchange at Doty. As I have three young kids (ages 4, 2 and 4 months), the basement space is at a premium and all I can really justify right now is about a two-foot shelf on the Manistique wall and a few inches on the rest.

As you know, fantasizing about the layout is just as much fun as building it, and as you can tell I am more into the fantasy stage than the building stage right now. My goal is to start laying track by the end of this year, but who knows. It is a little hard to justify spending much time or money on it right now with the growing family. Also, a lot depends on reading Hugh's manuscript and what really happened on the M&LS, as I would like to be pretty close to prototypical.

Prior to writing the next letter to the editor I had built my first boxcar for my model railroad, using a set of decals he had sent to me. It really wasn't an appropriate model freight car for me as it was too "modern" of a car and the decals were put together by him as sort of a "what if" the M&LS survived longer and had a fleet of boxcars, what would they look like? Below is a photograph of this freight car.

April 30, 1990

Dear Editor,

Just thought I'd write to transmit the enclosed photograph of M&LS #25000. I thought it turned out quite well. I chose a Roundhouse 50-foot boxcar and the color is Floquil Dark Green. The car is too modern for my model railroad but it is in service on a friend's railroad in exchange for one of his road's boxcars more suitable to my circa-1953 era. Thanks a lot for the decals, as it was a lot of fun building it and fits in perfectly in my friend's layout.

With respect to my layout, I finished the benchwork and have most of the rolling stock I need to get started. I used the two extra M&LS initials and numbers from the decal set you sent to do two gondolas and two flat cars for

M&LS, which will be all of my M&LS rolling stock. I decaled up two hoppers for Ann Arbor. From the Soo Line Historical Society contact I got a lot of good information on Duluth, South Shore & Atlantic Railroad rolling stock in the late 40's and early 50's for my DSS&A interchange. He also said that Ann Arbor routed a lot of hopper cars to Marquette via M&LS and LS&I for coal loading for the Ann Arbor carferry's coal appetite. That will be a regular move on my layout. Now I am saving up my money for track and switches.

November 6, 1990

Dear Editor,

Just thought I would update you on the M&LS.

When jumping into building a model railroad, I tried to analytically plan out my course of action. I have a lot of friends that have excellent model railroads but I never really involved myself in anything but the operation of them. I knew that I was going to model the M&LS and that it was going to have to fit into my basement in such a way that the kids could still use the basement pretty much undisturbed until they grew a little older. One reason I picked the M&LS was because it was a shortline and this fit in well with the physical constraints of money, skill (or lack thereof) and sharing the room in the basement with the kids.

I decided to do a U-shaped layout around the basement with one twenty-foot leg being a bench top eighteen inches wide and the other leg and the bottom of the U just six inches wide except for a widening at the corner. The 20-foot by 18-inch bench would be the City of Manistique and would include a three-track yard, a carferry slip, an engine house and some industries. The approximately 24 remaining feet of six-inch shelf would essentially be the mainline to the LS&I interchange at Doty at the end of the line. The expanded corner could be a town, probably Stueben, with one or two minor industries.

Putting in the benchwork was pretty easy once I thought it out, made the decision and purchased the material. All I used were 2 X 4's for the frame under Manistique with ½ inch plywood as the surface top. The rest, being the mainline, was eight-foot sections of 2 X 6's with a plywood expansion at the corner. The 2 X 6's were supported by shelving angle irons screwed into the cement walls of the basement, which were surprisingly very sturdy.

I figured that the 2 X 6's will largely be supporting a single track mainline with a short run-around and siding at the DSS&A interchange at Shingleton and a two-track stub yard at the end of the line for the interchange siding with the LS&I.

Needless to say, the benchwork only took me a few hours to build though I did do it in three parts: Manistique's benchwork, followed by the plywood sheet for Manistique, followed by the mainline on the other two walls. I used plastic expander plugs for attaching either the 2 X 4's or the angle irons to the cement walls of the basement with lag or small wood screws, carriage bolts for the rest of the Manistique benchwork and wood screws for the plywood.

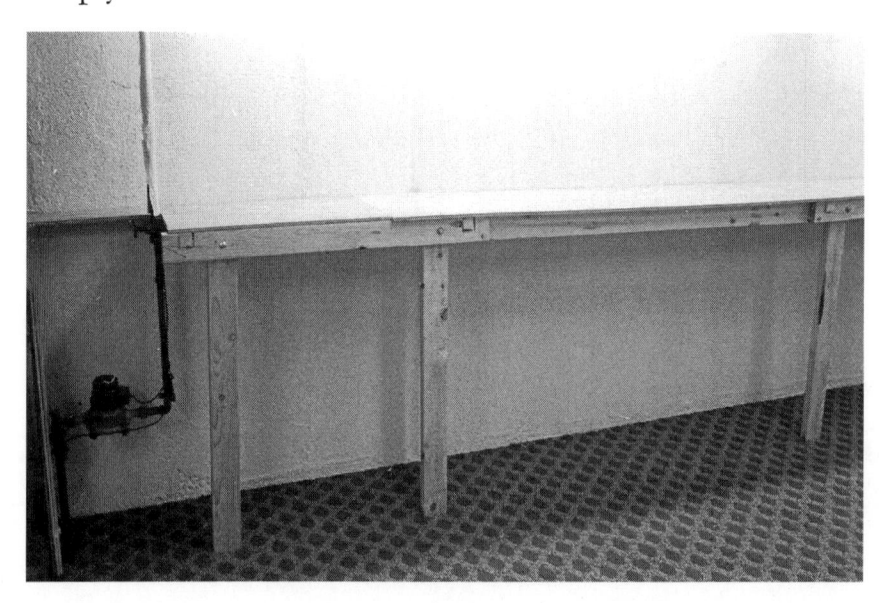

I did all of the above last Spring before the good weather hit and I knew I would be getting busy with outdoor work. Before and while this was going on I also started working on buying some rolling stock. This was the fun part as it gave me the excuse to visit all the hobby shops in the area. I figured that my layout could support between 50 and 60 freight cars. I tried to limit myself to buying various types of freight cars from interchanging railroads, Wisconsin and Michigan railroads in general. I even got into decaling undecorated freight cars.

The decaling efforts went into decaling unique Michigan railroads like the DSS&A, Pere Marquette, Detroit & Mackinac, Ann Arbor, GTW and, of course, M&LS. This was because not many commercial model railroad companies build small, somewhat obscure, railroad freight cars. As far as I could tell, M&LS only had a few of its

own cars in the early 1950's (I am technically modeling it in 1953, the first full year of dieselization), probably just flat cars and gondolas for wood shipments, so I did decal up two 40' gondolas, two 40' flats and two 30' flat cars, all painted black, for M&LS. The 30' flat cars will probably be used for idler cars for switching the carferry. Decaling was a lot of fun and rather easy, even for an amateur like me.

Right now I have quite a few freight cars, much more than I can use for my small layout. Recent issues by Bev-Bel of Ann Arbor, DSS&A, Copper Range and Detroit & Mackinac boxcars as well as Soo Line Historical Society boxcar issues this year really helped out the cause. Your book on Ann Arbor freight cars also was a great help in decaling three Ann Arbor hoppers (one of each kind: ribbed, paneled and composite) and two gray covered hoppers.

With respect to purchasing motive power for my layout, Atlas Tool Company really came through in a timely manner with their release of Alco S-2 and S-4 switchers this year. As you know, M&LS's only diesel engine was a black and yellow Alco S-3. I purchased an Atlas NYC S-2 (because it was black), ordered from Atlas an undecorated cab and S-4 trucks ($10.50), painted the undecorated cab engine black and painted out the white frame and pilot striping on the NYC engine and applied the AARRTHAssoc decals for M&LS's S-3 and, presto, an almost duplicate of the M&LS's #1 (except for the larger S-2/4 radiator).

I even purchased the correct spark arrester for the stack and put it on sideways as the M&LS did. Of course, pictures of M&LS #1 published in *The Double A* as well as painting diagrams in some of the articles in *The Double A* helped.

The month of October was set aside for putting the finishing touches on the benchwork and the basement before the laying of track. I purchased eight 4' shop lights and evenly spaced them across the basement ceiling to give the basement more light. I also purchased two 8' shop lights and suspended these directly above the 20' by 18" bench that is to be Manistique as this was where most of the action was going to take place.

Next, I decided to cover the entire benchwork surface with tan shingle paper. On a trip (pilgrimage?) to Manistique this past summer to trace the M&LS right-of-way and to probe around the property (nothing much left except for the engine house and carferry slip: the right-of-way is now a snowmobile path and thus still there), I noticed that underneath the tracks was sand the entire length of the railroad. Because of that and the fact that the track did not look like it ever had much ballast, I picked tan shingle paper as my base instead of using cork under the track for the roadbed. I purchased a roll of tan shingle paper and stapled it to the top of all the benchwork. It doesn't look bad and, with some ballasting of the track and some landscaping, it should work out real well.

The month of November was dedicated to deciding on the track layout, buying track and switches and then laying the track. This is where cost started becoming an issue. I decided on using Code 100 Atlas flex-track for my entire track work and Shinahorah turnouts. Since I was going to just be operating the Atlas Alco switcher and maybe other short-wheelbase engines and I do have space limitations I decided to go with #4 turnouts. Another reason for using the #4's was that a model railroad friend of mine had a dozen or so used #4's that he had no need for on his layout and the price was right. He also purchased quite a number of Nickel Plate #5 wyes on sale (made by Shinahorah) and offered them to me at a great price so I decided to work a number of these into the layout instead of using turnouts as switches. These wyes, though not prototypical, are great space-savers on a small layout like mine when used instead of a turnout.

I spent one uninterrupted evening laying the track in early November and finished the entire layout, except for laying some of the industrial trackage in Manistique as I was not quite sure what buildings will be located where yet.

I decided to have two industrial tracks coming off the mainline and yard in Manistique. From looking at photocopies of old maps sent to me by Hugh Hornstein, I was able to get an idea of what industries were switched by M&LS in Manistique. I have been purchasing the new Walthers Cornerstone Series buildings, as they appear to fit fairly well with the type of industries the M&LS serviced in Manistique.

The Intrastate Bulk Fuel Distribution Center put out by Walthers worked out well, as there was a bulk fuel industry on the M&LS. The American Mill Works also worked out well for my layout as there was a cooperage company and a box company on the M&LS at one time and wood products were a major part of the Upper Peninsula economy. The Cornerstone Water Street Freight House will turn out to be an industry on my layout instead of a freight house. I would like one major industry and

Manistique does have Manistique Pulp and Paper Company. Though I believe that Soo Line actually switched the Pulp and Paper plant it was close enough to M&LS trackage that I will probably make it an on-line industry on my layout and will modify the Water Street Freight House to make it into the Manistique Pulp and Paper Company. In addition to these three industries, I will also have a lumber yard, a coal yard and a sand and gravel/building supply company where I can run hoppers and covered hoppers with gravel and sand to (I have to find a use for my Ann Arbor covered hoppers) as well as boxcars with cinder blocks, bagged cement, bricks and other supplies.

The only problem with the Cornerstone series of buildings is that they are very large buildings and thus take up a lot of room on the layout. I may be able to squeeze a couple more industries in along the wall in Manistique if I use just storefront-type structures (or should I say storeback) or wall murals but all I really want is four or five industries because as far as I can tell that is all that M&LS serviced there in the early 1950's.

I also wanted an engine house for my railroad. In the early 1950's it appears that M&LS had a roundhouse with a turntable. Sometime in the 1960's or so it burnt down and was replaced by a one-stall building and the turntable was removed. Though I would like a roundhouse and turntable, space does not permit it so I purchased a two-locomotive engine house by International Hobby Corp. and can use the second stall in case I ever decide to run a second engine for operational purposes. I did pick 1953, the first full year of dieselization on the M&LS, so I could run a steam engine along side of the diesel, though I doubt M&LS ever ran their steam engines after the S-3 diesel arrived. The IHC engine house was much shorter than many of the others on the market, especially compared to the Cornerstone enginehouse that Walthers is coming out with that is essentially their American Millworks building, a very long structure.

In addition to the industries located in Manistique, I plan on having a short siding for the town of Hiawatha and a run-around track servicing some industries in Stueben. Both will be located in the corners of the layout. Hiawatha in real life in the early years had a three-mile spur off the mainline to reach it but in the 1950's was reduced to just a siding that, according to Hugh Hornstein, occasionally received a car for hay loading. I will probably just put a loading ramp there and set-off an occasional car for pulpwood or hay loading or what-have-you. Stueben will probably also get a loading ramp and I purchased a Helgan saw mill which fits in the corner perfectly and fits in well with the lumber trade of the U.P.

I spent hours agonizing on how the track should be laid out. Basically, the layout starts at two stub tracks extending from the end of Manistique. This serves as the carferry. I am only planning on switching five or six cars at a time from the carferry. Someday I may actually have a carferry but for now the carferry is these two tracks.

From the carferry the track angles across the width of the benchwork with a one-track siding or boat yard located along this stretch. The M&LS had a small boat yard at their carferry slip. It then straightens out and becomes a three-track yard with a three-way switch at either end and a crossover between the middle and outside track halfway down the yard. A switch is located at the inside track of this yard to enter the industrial trackage and also a switch comes off this track to the engine house and facilities. Between the Boat Yard and the Main Yard another industrial spur comes off the main line and will service two industries.

At the north end of the yard in Manistique the track starts at a wye, which bends to the left for the Soo Line, interchange track and to the right for the mainline winding around the corner of the basement. At the end of the curve is another wye connecting the mainline curving out of Manistique with the mainline to Stueben. The right side of the wye is a short stub track that will be Hiawatha Spur.

The mainline continues across the basement wall on the 2 X 6 shelf eight feet until it reaches the other corner where two more wyes allow it to curve to the right for the mainline and to the left for a wide siding that will be the industrial track for the town of Stueben as well as a run-around track, if needed.

Along the 2 X 6 shelf that runs approximately 18 feet along the final leg of the "U," the mainline encounters another run-around that has a spur coming off it at the south end. This is the town of Shingleton and the spur is the Duluth South Shore & Atlantic Railroad interchange track. The north end of the siding is another wye switch followed by three feet of a single track mainline again until it encounters another wye switch splitting into a two-track three-foot long stub yard that is the LS&I interchange and the end of the line at Doty.

All trains will be a maximum of five cars in length. I tried to make all sidings, yards and interchange tracks at least three feet long to accommodate five-car trains with a caboose and a locomotive. The only exception is the carferry, which is two tracks about a foot and a half long, each which, between the two of them, will easily accommodate five cars.

Next on my learning curve, now that the track is laid, is electricity. I know nothing about power packs and transformers and wiring and blocks so this is going to be the hard part. I am already thinking about it and asking questions so it will be worked out before too long. After this will be figuring out how to operate the railroad prototypically. This means waybills, rolling stock, car flow etc. Then will come the detail work, landscaping, ballasting, etc. If I think too far in advance I get overwhelmed. Good thing it is a small layout.

December 10, 1990

Dear Editor,

Thought I'd further update you on my adventures modeling the Manistique & Lake Superior Railroad.

When I last wrote, I was just getting ready to wire the model railroad up. Or, should I say, I was educating myself on how to wire it up.

After talking to all my railroad friends, I figured out exactly what I wanted to do, how to do it and what materials I needed to do what I needed to do. The threshold question was how many engines did I want to be able to operate at one time? Originally I said that is an easy question: one engine as that is all the M&LS ever operated at one time. This answer would have made my life very simple. However, my friends pointed out to me what if I ever wanted to run an interchange using the interchanging railroad's engine into my yard? Or, more importantly, if I only ran one engine I could never have much of an operating session as I could only have one person operating the railroad at a time.

Well, their logic (or self-invitation) prevailed and I decided to be able to operate two engines. Heck, I am modeling the year 1953 when M&LS dieselized and I could rationalize that they did run their old Consolidation type steam locomotive and their new S-3 diesel switcher together, at least for awhile. And it would allow me to invite at least two people over at a time to operate. Once my friends found out that I swallowed the "more than one engine" routine they quickly convinced me that wiring the railroad up for three was just as easy as for two. Heck, I could always say the M&LS was borrowing Ann Arbor Railroad locomotives. So that is how I ended up answering the threshold question: I will wire up my railroad so as many as three locomotives can operate at the same time. Little did I know at the time how that would complicate my life and triple my expenditures.

A modern corollary to the "how many engines do you want to operate at a time" question is "do you want conventional power or Dynatrol?" Conventional power, as I found out, is where you individually wire blocks of track and control, which throttle feeds power to these blocks by toggle switches. Dynatrol is a block-less operating scheme so that two or more locomotives can occupy and run on the same piece of track independently of each other. I have a couple friends with Dynatrol layouts and they are great to operate on. Very prototypical and easy to use. However, it is very expensive, complicated to put the transmitters into the engines, touchy and, overall, way above my head and income. For my layout, conventional power should work out just fine for starters and if I want I can someday switch over to Dynatrol.

The first problem encountered with the decision to operate more than one engine was figuring out the blocks. On my small layout, to be able to operate three engines at one time I would need 28 blocks. What this means is 28 toggle switches, close to 1000 feet of wire, three transformers and three throttles/rectifiers. This adds up to a lot of money. All so I can have my friends over to play on my railroad in a manner that they are use to (i.e., being busy all night). Basically, you isolate all runarounds, industrial areas and yard tracks as well as logical sections of mainline by insulating them from the adjacent track one of two ways: using plastic rail joiners or by cutting the track. I decided to cut the track for one simple reason: In my hurry to lay track (and at my excitement of having one full free evening to do it in November), I had not even given the least bit of thought to blocks or electricity, least of all to the "how many locomotives" question. By cutting blocks I can worry about this later though it is a less effective way of electrically insulating sections of track for blocks than the plastic rail joiners.

Once I figured out the blocks (actually my friend Ned figured this out for me), I started figuring out and buying the equipment to begin electrifying my railroad. Now, for some reason, most hobby shops seem to have forgotten that all this electrical stuff is part of the hobby. They carry little in the way of transformers, toggles, wire and throttles and know little about it. My experience was that you have to go to an electrical supply store. First I went to a Radio Shack but that was not really the place to go. Radio Shack may have what you need but they do not really seem to understand the needs of a model railroader and you can get a much better price elsewhere.

I then went to an electronics store in Livonia, Michigan and they were the right place. I purchased 30 double pole/double throw toggles for $2.15 each, three 18 volt, 2 amp step down transformers at $16.00 each and eight rolls of spools of 24-guage tinned single stranded wire in two colors in 100 foot spools for $10 each (also available in 1000 foot spools for a little less per foot).

Purchasing a throttle, though, does take you back to the hobby shop. A friend of mine, who models a fictitious railroad, recently purchased some throttles from GML Enterprises out of Oxford, Michigan. Gene Lewis builds them out of his home and they are great. They come with a built-in rectifier (beats me what this is but you need it and usually it is separate from the throttle), a small hand-throttle and 15 foot of cord. All you do is hook it up to the transformer and to the tracks and you are ready to go. Not one to do much shopping and knowing that something works well when he sees it, I ordered three of these throttles at $40 a piece (why did I ever let them talk me into running more than one locomotive at a time?).

Once I purchased all my electrical equipment I was anxious to start installing it. The first thing I had to do was to build a control board to put all the toggles in along with a track diagram to show what blocks the toggles control. I found a scrap piece of 1/8" plywood that I hinged to the benchwork in front of Manistique yard and painted it black with white 3/16" chart tape being used for the track diagram. The whole thing was over-coated with polyurethane when I completed it. Surprisingly, this step was very easy and was necessary to start my wiring project.

I also quickly realized that I somehow had to hide all the wiring, transformers, rectifiers and the back of the toggle switches so that the kids did not get into them and mess them up, or worse yet, get shocked. Behind the toggle box I boxed in a portion of the benchwork with removable sides where all my exposed electrical equipment will be hidden yet easily accessible, if needed.

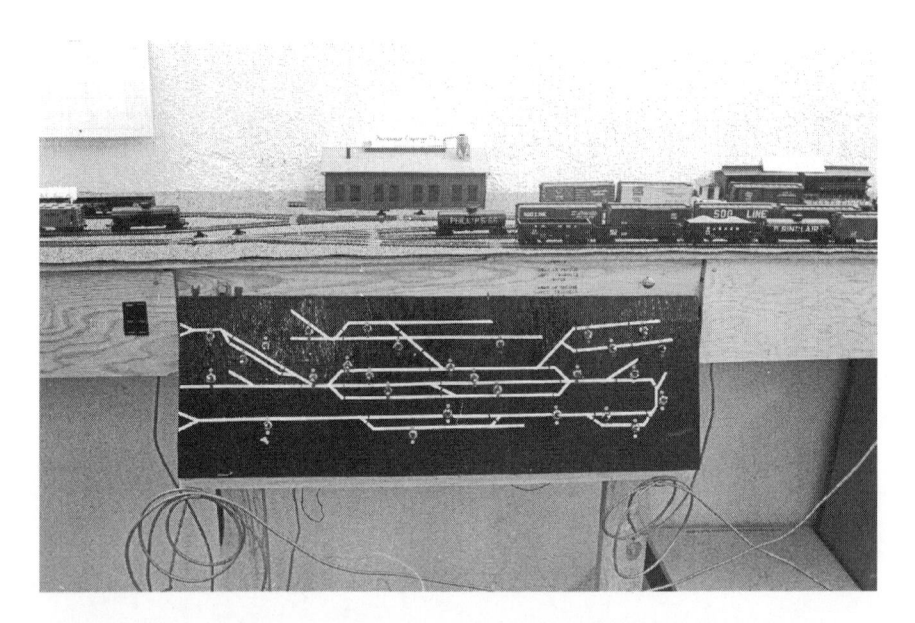

Next was drilling holes into the control board for the toggles and inserting the toggles. The hardest thing about this was lining up the toggles so they represented a schematic of the track layout so, at a glance, you could see which block you were routing which power pack to.

Then came running the wires from each block to the right toggle in the control box. I used 24-gauge wire in black and red colors. Drilling a hole into the top of the benchwork, running a black and red wire into their holes and soldering them to the outside rail of the track and then running the wire to the toggle was a simple enough task. However, it was time-consuming since there were 28 blocks, some being 35 feet away from the control box. A few tips: use flux on the side of the rail before soldering, always solder the wires to the outside of the rails so the flanged wheels on the freight cars do not hit it, give yourself an extra foot or so of wire and have at least two times more wire than you think you need. I thought I would need 400 feet of wire and ended up using over 800 feet. This may sound like obvious tips but I learned them all the hard way. After the blocks were wired up, I went back and filed down all the solder spots so a freight car would run smooth over them.

Next came wiring up the transformers and throttles. The transformers I bought were 18-volt step down AC at 2 amps. They had no instructions or inscriptions on them to tell you which wires were input wires and which were output. One side had three wires, the other two. Logically, I figured the three-wire side was input as the middle, striped, wire was probably the ground, and I put a plug on them and wired the two wires on the other side to the rectifier. Wrong. I think a dimmed all the lights in the neighborhood that night when I plugged it in. The best advice is make sure you know which wires are input and which are output before you do anything.

Amazingly, I did not blow-up anything after that and the next night, after calling the electronics store to find out which wires are input and which are output, I switched the wiring around. For now, I am just running a heavy-duty extension cord from a wall socket to behind the control board and am plugging the three transformers into that for power. The transformers are merely screwed into the benchwork. Someday I will wire it a little more professionally with a switch that has a light so I can see that the power is on.

The GML throttles are made so the rectifier portion just screws into and suspends from the benchwork. There is a 15-foot cord coming from this and then the nice small hand-held throttles. I am planning on using Velcro to stick the throttles to the side of the benchwork when they are not in use. The two wires from the transformer merely are attached to the input side (clearly marked) on the rectifier. The wires going to the track then go to each individual toggle.

I connected the throttle to the toggles as follows: First, I have three throttles and only double-throw toggles. What I did was assign blue and red pack to the carferry, boat yard, Manistique yard and the city of Manistique. Then I assigned the blue pack and the yellow pack to the rest of the railroad, being the mainline from just outside of the yard at Manistique all the way to the end of the line at Doty. This way I can have someone switching the carferry or the main yard on red pack, someone switching the town of Manistique on blue pack and someone taking a train out of town on the yellow pack. When the outbound train on yellow pack returns to Manistique the train being operated by the blue throttle will have to be isolated so the yellow throttle man can throw the yard toggles from blue to yellow and bring his train into the yard. All the while the red pack guy can keep operating as long as he doesn't run on the same blocks as the blue pack train.

Since it would be physically impossible to run wires from about 20 toggles to the hook-up on the rectifier, what I did was run a bus-bar that was wired to the rectifier and then soldered the wires from all the toggles to that bus-bar so that when all the toggles were thrown into the red position, the positive and negative wires from the toggles went to the positive and negative bus-bar for red throttle. What I used for a bus-bar was a piece of flex-track with one rail being for the positive wire and the other rail for the negative. The ties helped in keeping the wires separated for each toggle and also helped in nailing the ends of the bus-bar to the backsides of the control box. As I have three throttles, I used three pieces of flex-track for bus-bars, one for each throttle.

A few more tips at this point. The wiring is best if you consistently use one color wire for positive and one color wire for negative and one side of the track and toggles for positive and the other side of the track for negative. Also, when the toggle is thrown upwards, it connects the wires at the bottom of the toggle, opposite of what you would think. The center wire positions on the toggles is the track wire position where the wires run from the track in the block you are controlling to the toggle and the top and bottom wire position on the toggle are for the two throttles you are running to that block. Again, obvious tips that I learned the hard way.

On December 10, 1990 at approximately 9:20 pm, I went back down to the railroad, changed the input and output wires on the transformers, put an Atlas RS-1 locomotive on the track, plugged in the power, turned on the switch, threw a toggle, twisted the throttle knob and watched in disbelief as the engine rolled merrily down the track in a controlled manner. I felt like a rocket scientist watching his creation soar successfully off into space. All the theory worked in practice and the M&LS was in business.

The moral of this story is that if I can do it, anyone can.

What's next? Operating the M&LS and the concurrent picking of rolling stock, typing cards for each car and destination waybills, train flow and all of the really fun stuff.

February 10, 1991

Dear Editor,

Here is another update on my adventures in model railroading.

January 1, 1991 was a historic day. The Manistique & Lake Superior Railroad ran again.

In November, I succumbed to pressure from my model railroad friends to pick a date for the first operating session on my not-yet built railroad (heck, I did not even have the track laid yet). So I reluctantly said January 1.

The good thing about peer pressure is that it can give you the motivation to do the impossible. I spent a frenzied month of December wiring up the railroad, picking out and finishing freight cars to run on the railroad, building structures, figuring out car routings and typing cards for each freight car and waybills for routings for each type of freight car, fine tuning the railroad so that trains would operate over it at least half-way decently, etc. I did not even have the wiring done so I could run a train until December 10th.

But everything fell into place and at 11 am on New Years Day, 1991 (a morning session so as not to interfere with all the football games that day), three of the best and most experienced model railroaders I knew walked down into the basement and the M&LS was reborn in HO scale.

I wasn't too sure whether we would actually run trains that first day or just look at the railroad. After about a half-hour introducing and examining the railroad, I suggested we try to run some trains and the rest is history. The three pro's got right into the saddle and began running the M&LS like they had been there operating many times. Ned was the yardmaster and began making a road train for Doty and points in between. Jim began pulling cars out of the industrial area and, when the road train was made up, Bill took it out on the mainline.

About forty-five minutes later, Bill and Jim had completed their duties and Ned had another industrial job and a road job ready to go and the two crews switched jobs, Bill taking the industrial job and Jim the road job. The whole time I was the superintendent, attending to minor problems, answering questions and generally just watching my railroad work.

After everyone finished running their second train we called it quits, cracked open a bottle of champagne, and reviewed the operation. It was a real joy to be there watching these three experienced model railroaders running my railroad and being kept busy doing so for almost two hours. One full year of work, almost to the day, resulted in an operating model railroad. What an accomplishment.

It was interesting how my crew actually operated the railroad versus how I envisioned it being operated. Ned used the boat yard run-around as the arrival and departure track for all trains instead of the third track of the yard. This gave him more room for his work and allowed crews to take power to and from the trains and engine house without interfering with him. I thought they would run into the third track, uncouple, the yardmaster would take the train away, and they would then run the power light to the engine house but that proved too cumbersome for a three-man operation.

I also figured that road trains would be all DSS&A interchange or all LS&I interchange trains with an occasional train with cars for Hiawatha and Stueben sidings. In fact, the road trains had cars for all four road destinations and thus did work all the way, which was probably more prototypical and definitely more fun for the road crew. I also thought that the Manistique Industrial Track, the South Industrial Track and the Soo Line Interchange would all be separate jobs. The way it worked out was that the industrial crew would have cars for all three and would thus work all three areas in Manistique.

The main reason for these operational changes was that there were not enough cars in the freight yard for there to be five-car trains destined to a specific location, such as the

LS&I interchange, especially when three operators were working. It worked out much better to send a road train out or an industrial job out whenever there were five cars for the road or industries and this way was probably more prototypical. I have found, though, that when I operate the railroad myself with one engine I often do runs with all LS&I cars or all DSS&A cars because there aren't two additional crew to keep busy.

We did not have a boat train during the session, which may have been a fluke or may mean I do not have enough cars routed to the boat. I figured that at least one pull of the carferry would occur a session, if not two or three. I figured one mainline trip and one industrial switch job would encompass one day's activity and that probably only one boat a day maximum would call in the early 1950's. My waybill destinations may need some tweaking.

The biggest problems during my operating session were that most of the freight cars had weight, wheel gauge and coupler height problems and this was further exaggerated by some rough track work in areas. I spent the month of January going over each freight car on the layout making sure the coupler height was correct using a Kadee Couple Height gauge, an NMRA gauge for checking the wheel gauge of each axle and a postal scale for checking the weight of each car. It is a rare car that has all its wheels in gauge and all cars are way too light right out of the box. I figured that a 40-foot car should weigh four ounces and all others should weigh at least 3 3/4 ounces, without a load. To this end, I purchased a box of weight strips with sticky backing that was scored and could be cut in 1/4-ounce segments. Most cars needed between a half an ounce to an ounce to meet my weight requirements.

I also subjected all my freight cars to a roll test. I have a slight grade on about eight feet of my railroad and all cars should roll freely on their own from the top to the bottom of the grade and make the curve at the bottom of the grade without derailing. I found that almost all Athearn cars had no problem doing this after they have been prepped and most MDC cars were OK but only about half of the Walthers cars can do it. My hunch is that the trucks on the Walthers cars are no good and at some point I may replace all of them with Athearn trucks.

I have also been weathering each car as I do the above work. As much as I like the way they look new, the freight cars look much more prototypical weathered. All they really seem to need is something to take off the shine but I have gone from merely doing that in some cases to more severe weathering depending on the type and age of car. The flats and gondolas got a good dose of "Rust-All," a commercial product my hobby shop carries. It is a liquid that is brushed on and it gets into all the corners and crannies and looks like rust when it dries. The more applied, the rustier it looks. I have found this works best with black cars though a brown car that you do not want too weathered does well too. A part of a Rust-All kit you can buy includes a white and a black liquid. The white is a random flat, which does great just taking the shine off the cars. I have been using it moderately on newer cars and heavily on others to give them a dusty appearance, especially on coal and gravel hoppers. The black is suppose to bring out highlights such as rivets after the other two liquids are used but I also used it on cars to dirty up the white lettering. The fourth bottle is dirt for dust that I have not used yet. They also sell each bottle separately.

In light of how weathered covered hoppers in cement service get (as can be seen from the Ann Arbor Freight Car book), I decided to use pulverized gray chalk to weather the eight covered hoppers I have on my railroad. Applied with a brush, this method worked out real well weathering these cars and all of my boxcars.

The operating session was great in pointing out some changes that could be made to facilitate the operation of three engines at once. Since we had a yardmaster and a industrial switch crew busy all the time, it was inconvenient that the road crew could not run his trains on yellow pack (the road pack) into the yard but, instead, had to wait outside of town until someone let him use their pack to bring a train in. To remedy this, I rewired some sections of track in the yard so that three packs can be accessed. This way a yard train can come right into Manistique yard and take his engine to the roundhouse afterwards, all on yellow pack.

The way I did this was to have the toggles on certain blocks in Manistique be so that toggle down is not red pack but is to a separate toggle located on the far corner of the toggle panel. The direction of this separate toggle, either to red or yellow pack, then controls that block. This way I was able to stay with my two-way toggles and just control whether it is on red or yellow pack by the way the side toggle is thrown. I wired up all of Manistique Yard, Boat Yard, engine house tracks and leads and all the mainline trackage going through Manistique to the carferry this way. It was a very simple correction to what turned out to be my only major wiring miscalculation.

My crews also had some ideas as to adding some trackage in Manistique so that they can switch industries without interfering with the yardmaster's switching duties. Though I am considering these I am always trying to keep in mind that I am modeling a small, sleepy, one engine railroad and to stretch it by operating three engines at once would cause some of these operational problems.

I ended up having the following industries on the railroad on my first operation day: City Fuel and Oil Co., Schoolcraft Supply Co., Manistique Pulp and Paper Co., Manistique Cooperage Co., Goodwillie Brothers Box Co., Girvin Coal Co., Brown Lumber Co. and Stueben Sawmill. In addition, there was a ramp at Hiawatha siding and at Stueben for miscellaneous freight. All of these except

Schoolcraft Supply and Stueben Sawmill were one-time industries in Manistique (though most were not active in my early 1950's era) though not all were necessarily serviced by the M&LS. During my visit to Manistique I did see a company that was alongside the one-time M&LS trackage

to the carferry that was an operating supply company selling bricks, stone and cement, and this gave me the idea for my Schoolcraft Supply Company and thus a place to route some of those covered hoppers.

City Fuel and Oil is the Walthers Cornerstone Intrastate Fuel Distributor structure and takes up to three tank cars and an occasional boxcar with supplies. Schoolcraft Supply is on the same spur (the South Industrial Spur I call it as it is off the mainline between the yard and the boat) and takes box cars and gondolas with bricks, bagged cement and stone as well as hoppers and covered hoppers for sand, gravel and cement on a ConCor gravel ramp and dump coming off the spur. Manistique Cooperage is the Walthers Cornerstone American Millwork building and takes box cars for shipping its products at a loading ramp located behind it in the Manistique Industrial Track.

Also on the same track are Brown Lumber (two Athearn lumberyards next to each other) and Goodwillie Brothers Box Company (a Walthers Cornerstone Water Street Freight House with a long loading dock all along the side). On its own long piece of track that is also used for shunting cars while servicing the other industries on the Manistique Industrial Track is Girvin Coal Co. which is a self-made ramp leading onto an elevated dump track I purchased. This is located right next to the engine house lead in case I ever run steam engines on the M&LS so they can be loaded with coal from there while at the engine house. Manistique Pulp and Paper right now is a two-track spur at the south end of the Manistique Industrial Track with one track for out-going boxcars and in-coming gondolas with pulpwood and the other track for covered hoppers with clay, tank cars with chemicals and hopper cars with coal. There is no building here yet and I am planning on reworking this rather large area on the railroad to extend one track along the wall with its own siding and to use those modular buildings the hobby shops have been carrying to build a very large structure flush with the wall to be the paper plant. The existing spur now used for covered hoppers and chemical cars may become Manistique Team Track, thus adding another industry.

Hiawatha siding just has a loading ramp and can accommodate two cars. Boxcars for hay loading and gondolas for pulpwood loading are routed there. Stueben siding has the sawmill (a Helgan structure) that takes flat cars and a loading ramp for pulpwood and general freight.

I spent a lot of time thinking about traffic flow and routings on the railroad. Hugh Hornstein says that a lot of bridge traffic ran across the M&LS between the Ann Arbor boat and the three interchanging railroads, Soo Line, Duluth South Shore & Atlantic and LS&I, and that a lot of traffic was routed between Soo Line and DSS&A over the

M&LS line. In later years, bridge traffic was just about the only traffic as there were few on-line industries shipping materials. Accordingly, I tried to prepare waybills with destinations along these lines. I have even been making lists of industries and commodities shipped to them that are on neighboring railroads that would have passed over M&LS. For instance, in 1953 White Pine Copper Mine and the city of White Pine in the western half of the Upper Peninsula was being built. DSS&A even built a 14-mile spur off their mainline to reach it. In the construction phase a ton of materials including cement, sand and steel were being shipped there over the DSS&A and so I presume a lot of cement in Ann Arbor covered hoppers came up that way via the M&LS. Also, the Mackinac Bridge was being built about that time so ditto for the sand, cement and steel moves to St. Ignace via DSS&A. DSS&A serviced the now-closed Raco Air Force Base so I have airplane and jet fuel routed over the M&LS. There were pulp and paper plants all over the state so I have a lot of pulpwood-loaded gondolas, clay-loaded covered hoppers and chemical cars routed to them as well as loaded boxcars routed back over M&LS. Hugh says that the Ann Arbor Railroad loaded almost all of their hopper cars with coal to keep their carferry fleet fueled at a coal loading facility in Marquette, so I have empty Ann Arbor and Wabash hoppers routed to the LS&I and loaded hoppers from the LS&I routed to M&LS. These are just a few examples to show the thought and fun that went into preparing my waybills and routing my freight cars. To me the most fun of a model railroad is operating it and so mine was built from day one as an operational railroad with historically-correct freight and routings.

Not so much fun was the actual typing of cards and waybills required for the M&LS to be an operational railroad. Each freight car had a library pocket card typed up for it showing its owner's name, its number, its type of car, a short description of the car and where it is to be routed to when empty. Ned actually had rubber stamps made for stamping the library pockets and all I had to do was type the correct information in on the pockets. I happened to have all this information in a computer program I created that shows this for every one of my freight cars and so all I did was run a hard copy report of this data and read off of that when I was typing. The library pocket card is perfect, as it is rigid enough for holding and taking abuse and can accommodate a 3 X 5 index card that is the waybill with routing information. When the car reaches its destination the waybill is either turned over or removed, depending on instructions on the waybill, resulting in a new destination either as a load or as an empty. All library pockets have an empty destination typed on them for when the index card waybill is removed it has one final destination.

Ned also had a stamp for the waybills. Most are loads so that the index card is removed from the library pockets after the car is delivered to its destination, resulting in the destination after delivery being the empty routing that appears on the library pocket card. Some waybill index cards are stamped on both sides, one stamp routing an empty card to, say, Manistique Pulp and Paper, for loading and the other side of the card for routing the loaded car from Manistique Pulp and Paper to its new destination. The stamp has areas for its destination, routing and lading. Destination can be as simple as just showing the interchanging railroad it is going to or as complicated as the name of a real industry in a certain town and all the railroad routings that it will need to get there, though only the M&LS-interchanged railroad appearing on the waybill is important to the crew. If it is an on-line industry that the car is going to, the waybill clearly states that the routing is via M&LS.

The waybills were color-coded according to type of freight car. Boxcar waybills have orange index cards, flats red, gondola yellow, reefers blue, hoppers white with black type and covered hoppers white with red type, and tank cars green. Library pockets, though clearly stating what type of car it is, are also color coded this way using a colored self-adhesive dot. Completed waybills, meaning the car has been delivered to the waybill's destination and the waybill says "remove," are removed. An empty car that has been delivered to its destination as typed on the library pocket gets a new waybill appropriate for the type of car it is and, to some extent, to the load it may have (for instance a hopper with a molded gravel load should not get a white waybill that has "coal" typed in as a lading). New waybills are stored by color in wooden pockets that are part of the fascia on front of the benchwork. Each industry, yard track or interchange also has a pocket for the cards that represent the cars currently in that industry or on that track.

An operating session begins with a yardmaster taking an engine to the south end of the yard and looking through the cards to see what cars in the yard go where. If he has five cars for any one destination (road train, Manistique industry or boat) he pulls them from the yard and puts them in the departure track for the crew and calls a crew to take a train. The crew then brings down an engine from the engine house with an unused throttle pack and couples onto the train and delivers the freight cars to the destinations called for on each of the waybills. The crew will remove the same number of cars from an industry or interchange that he is delivering to that industry or interchange, preferable the end ones, deliver the cars in his train waybilled for those industries and then take his "glories" or returning cars back to Manistique yard. The carferry is switched only when there are five cars going to it as, in real life, the carferry is always emptied of cars so five cars coming out requires five cars going in or else Manistique yard will get too full.

I currently have 65 freight cars out on the railroad broken down as follows: eight covered hoppers, ten hoppers (six with coal loads and four with gravel), twelve tank cars, twelve gondolas, five flats, one reefer and seventeen box cars. This way every interchange has five cars (except Soo, which can only handle four) and most industries or sidings have two or three cars per siding. Manistique yard has five or six cars on three of its four classification tracks. This way nothing is too crowded. When I add the team track and enlarge Manistique Pulp and Paper I will add two to five cars to the railroad, probably flats and reefers.

One final note to this update: As M&LS only had one locomotive I have taken modeler's liberty in having three locomotives on my layout. There is nothing like having a bunch of friends down operating your railroad and three locomotives being able to operate at the same time give three people something to do. I did model M&LS #1 fairly closely using an Atlas Alco S-2 with S-4 trucks and AAT&HA decals. I decided that the logical extension of M&LS motive power, in light of Ann Arbor RR's ownership of it, would be another Alco switcher for the yard and industrial switching work and an Alco RS-1 roadswitcher for the road trains. I already had an Atlas RS-1 and picked up an Atlas S-2 from a friend for a good price. I painted the RS-1 in the M&LS black and yellow scheme and numbered it #2 and, just to be different, painted and decaled the S-2 as Ann Arbor RR S-1 #3 and say that it is being borrowed from the parent. The beauty of the model railroad is that it can be operated with one, two or three locomotives and it operates just as well any way. It is nice to have those two extra locomotives in the engine house ready for use. The AARRT&HA decals for switchers really worked out great for them.

June 20, 1991

Dear Editor,

Though I am sure you wish I would just go away by now, I thought that I'd write another update on my trials and tribulations in modeling the Manistique & Lake Superior Railroad.

The biggest changes to the M&LS recently have all resulted from my experiences in operating it. Nothing like trial by error. At first I envisioned a sleepy, one locomotive railroad occasionally running a train, much like the prototype. Then, as you know, I let my friends talk me into a three-locomotive operation so I could have three people operating the railroad at one time. Since then I have been wrestling with how can I set up the railroad so it is still somewhat sleepy and a lot of fun with just one person operating yet have the capacity of keeping three people busy at once. Somewhat polar goals but I have found that a lot of enjoyment comes out of sharing the model railroad with your friends.

The first big operating change (other than the rolling stock and electrical work I wrote about last time) was to fix up some of the rough trackage. I was having problems with derailments at both of the corners of the layout, largely because the radius at both corners was fairly tight. It turns out that the benchwork was sagging at one corner because the plywood top extended beyond the 2 X 4 frame and needed bracing. Once that was done I re-laid the track and used insulated joiners for the block there instead of cutting blocks. The other corner had a wye switch at both ends causing the outside track of the run-around to have to make too severe of an angle so I replaced one of the wye switches with a #6 turnout which solved the problem in part, though not perfectly. I was also able to incorporate the displaced wye as a turnout on the runaround and that track is now the spur for Steuben Sawmill, the runaround being the siding for general freight going to Steuben. This made room for two more cars on the layout and added a little more freight car capacity to Steuben in addition to making the operation run smoother.

I also expanded the industrial trackage in Manistique to better use some space there. I took one of the two tracks for Manistique Pulp & Paper Co. and made it a team track. On the other I added a #4 switch and ran both tracks three feet along the back wall and called this Manistique Pulp & Paper. This increased my car capacity at MP&P by four cars and gave me room for two more cars at the team track.

I also had about three feet of space along the spur that now ended at Goodwillie Bros. Box Co. so I added a piece of flex-track ending in what I now call Berry Chemical Co., another industry once located in Manistique though probably never switched by M&LS. This allowed the addition of two extra cars to the layout.

I had planned on keeping only three of my four five-car Manistique Yard tracks full at any one time. I was quickly finding out, though, that at any one time I often did not have enough cars in Manistique Yard to make more than one five-car train going to any one of my crew assignments (boat, industrial, Soo Line interchange, road job). This was OK if only one person was operating at a time but was unsatisfactory when three people were operating, as often there would not be enough work to keep them busy. I decided to add five more cars to the layout, thus filling up Manistique Yard. Now there are always enough cars to make at least two, and often more, trains at any one time.

As a result of increasing the car capacity of my layout by fourteen cars I had to add fourteen cars to it. Now, one problem about my layout from day one is that I have quite a number of cars of railroads that happen to be favorites of mine. Because of this and the fact that the Ann Arbor Railroad owned M&LS, I have three boxcars, three hoppers and five covered hoppers all painted up for Ann Arbor. I also have four Detroit & Mackinac cars, two DSS&A boxcars, two LS&I boxcars, four Soo Line, three Wabash (all hoppers), a Pere Marquette, a GTW, E&LS, GB&W, Algoma Central and other cars from local railroads. Except for gondolas and flat cars I have very few non-local freight cars on the railroad.

I also only had one reefer on the railroad, largely because

I did not have any industries on the layout that received or shipped perishables. Well, with the addition of the team track and the realization that Hiawatha and Steuben siding could realistically receive reefers for unloading at the ramps and the need for fourteen more cars, I decided to add four more reefers. I also was finding out that, surprisingly, I had too few boxcars for the industries that I had. So to remedy this I added five more boxcars. I made sure that all ten of these cars were of non-local railroads and I also tried to make them non-Athearn produced cars to get some height variation in my rolling stock (six of the cars are old Train-Miniature cars now sold by Walthers, one is double sheathed wood, four are X-29 type cars and one is a steel reefer).

As to the remaining four cars, my two oldest children (ages 5 and 2) have wanted to get involved in my hobby so I let them build some freight cars. I took them to the hobby shop and let them pick any undecorated Athearn car then pick out some decals and helped them build, paint and decal them. So far we added three cars to the layout this way, one triple-dome tank car, one boxcar and a hopper.

I also decided to try the AAT&HAssoc recipe for kit-bashing an Ann Arbor Railroad streamlined caboose as M&LS did have one. Up to this point I was using an old Central Valley side-door caboose based on a 36' boxcar that I had built years ago (my first adventure into model railroading) as the M&LS caboose. M&LS used an ex-Wabash wooden caboose built from a boxcar for years before the AA steel one came over so I was at least in the ballpark. I also found that the potential existed for having two road trains running at one time and I therefore needed two cabooses. The instructions published in *The Double A* were great and I built a nice looking caboose for around $10 and just a couple nights' work. My first kit-bashing project.

One reason I decided to model the M&LS was that I wanted an Upper Peninsula railroad and one of the reasons I wanted an Upper Peninsula railroad was because I was fascinated by the movement of iron ore from mines to ships. Needless to say I almost fell over when, after picking M&LS as my railroad, Hugh Hornstein wrote to tell of a short, unsuccessful iron ore operation over M&LS! Without going into too much detail, Ford Motor was looking for a way to ship ore from Humboldt Mine on the LS&I in the Upper Peninsula (Ford was part owner or had some connection with the mine) to its Dearborn River Rouge Plant in Michigan's lower peninsula outside of Detroit via rail in the winter without going through Chicago. Though it sounds like they gave up after about a week, Ford did ship 40 to 50 loaded iron ore cars a day over M&LS from LS&I, across Lake Michigan on the Ann Arbor carferries, over the Ann Arbor Railroad to Diane and from there to the DT&I which delivered the ore directly to the plant sometime in the mid-1960's. Apparently the physical condition of the M&LS tracks could not handle such heavy cars in such a quantity and derailments were so frequent that they gave up after just a couple attempts. However, in the pretend world of model railroading this has now become a common move over the 1950's HO M&LS in my basement. Ah, the poetic license given to model railroaders.

I bought eight MDC LS&I 28' iron ore hopper cars and shuttle them between Doty and the carferry in a unit train. So as to avoid laying any new tracks to accommodate these cars, what I do is only send a train to Doty to interchange with the LS&I when there are five cars going there (eight ore cars equal the length of five freight cars). The train exchanges the five general freight cars for the eight iron ore hoppers and takes the ore back to Manistique. Since they are all for the boat, this triggers an immediate boat train pull, adding five general freight cars from the boat to the layout in exchange for the eight ore cars. It works out real well and iron ore trains are a unique operation even in such a small scale.

In order to slow down the turn-around of the ore train off the carferry and so as not to displace five other cars from the railroad, I extended the carferry so it is two three-foot tracks. Whenever there are five cars for the carferry at Manistique yard the track not last pulled at the carferry is pulled. This way the ore train does not come off the carferry with the next carferry switch. It is especially satisfying that there was a real life basis for this operation, even if it was a dismal failure.

I also added two MDC 30' flat cars to the layout to act as idler cars for pulling the carferry. One is painted black and lettered for M&LS and the other is Tuscan red and lettered for Ann Arbor. In Stan Mailer's book on the Green Bay & Western Railroad, in the Ann Arbor Railroad chapter, there is a large photograph of M&LS's consolidation switching the carferry at Manistique. The idler cars were old flat cars loaded with wheels and trucks for weight, I presume, and at least one was an Ann Arbor flat. I have not yet added junk to mine but I did have to weight them up a bit using buckshot glued in the spaces in the plastic frame. Due to lack of space they remain stored at the lead to the carferry where they are out of the way until they are needed.

I still needed a structure for Manistique Pulp & Paper Co. and also for Berry Chemical and basically wanted flat structures against the wall. I decided to go with a custom-built structure for Manistique Pulp & Paper using Design Preservation's modular system. I did have a portion of the structure come out from the wall and I run coal cars through it to the powerhouse and leave covered hoppers and tank cars inside of it for unloading. On the outside of the protruding section I have a small loading dock for incoming supplies in boxcars and along the wall portion of the building is a loading dock for the shipping department. A three-story office building is at the front of the structure and there is also a track for the pulpwood. With leftover pieces I built Berry Chemical. It cost me under $50 in total for two custom-built structures.

The next project on the list was the background scenery. This was really hanging me up for two reasons: One, I was reluctant to buy wood for this as it would be difficult to attach to the cement walls and I did not look forward to cutting it, priming it and then finding the right color blue to paint it. The second reason for the hang up was that I just was not finding commercially prepared background scenery or murals that I liked. None of the rural scenes were right for the cut-through-the-woods railroad I was modeling and the city/industrial murals were too industrial or urban for my small town of Manistique. Also, they were expensive. I figured I would have to spend around $300 for my background if I purchased commercially available backdrops. When operating at Bill's Erie & Michigan layout recently I looked carefully at what he had done. As part of his original layout he had a professional artist come in and paint some small town and rural background scenery. Mostly it was just a broad-brush stroke of pine trees and hills. Also, in some of his newer sections, Bill bought heavy light blue poster board and just tacked it up for the background.

   Now, the last thing I am is an artist. I cannot even draw a circle. But the estimated cost of doing the background the traditional way and the lack of satisfactory commercial backdrops allowed me come to the conclusion that it was worth a try to do the background scenery myself. So I drove out to the local artist supply store and bought eight 3' by 4' light blue poster board, a couple of wide brushes and various tubes of different colored acrylic paints. I cut the poster board in half length-wise at the store using their large paper cutter. Along the west wall of the layout the wall is drywall and I just stapled the poster board up. Along the cement south and east wall I attached patches of self-adhesive Velcro to the back of the poster board and pressed it against the wall. The cement wall side Velcro stuck well to the cement wall and I can easily peal off the poster board from the wall and reattach it using the Velcro.

My west and south wall is the rural mainline of my railroad and from my visit there last summer I noted that most of the railroad is merely cut through the woods. The further north the more pine trees there are and the further south the more deciduous trees plus some rolling farmland just north of Manistique. Using a dark brown paint, I made a ground base undulating from a half an inch to a couple inches along the bottom of the poster board along these two walls. This matches the color of my shingle paper base on the layout and acts as an extension of the right of way. Along the west wall all I did was broad-brush stroke conifer trees, one tree after another, varying the heights to give it some depth of field. At Shingleton, where the land is cleared out more, I did a small background line of conifers as if the tree line was out in the distance. In Steuben and Doty it is as if you are in the middle of the north woods. Along the south wall I painted a transition from conifers to deciduous trees and from woods to rolling farmland. The deciduous trees I made using a sponge to blot the paint on and used a lighter green paint than the dark conifers. The first stand of trees had both conifers and deciduous trees for the transition. The stands of deciduous trees had tree trunks painted in after the green paint was dry.

Manistique has a combination of deciduous trees and buildings in the background. I collected the advertising posters that Walthers came out with in advertising their four new Cornerstone Series buildings and cut out some of the pictures of buildings along with the background buildings and foreground scenery. These I pasted here and there, the smaller ones used to look like they are farther back and the larger ones to look like they are part of the immediate industrial scene. For example, Manistique Cooperage Co. is the American Millwork building and I cut out an angled view of it and placed it behind my structure to look like my building is one of two in the industry.

On either side of Berry Chemical I added cutouts of the

Intrastate Bulk Fuel Distributor to make Berry look like a big-time industry. In between the cutouts I just painted more deciduous trees, as that was the way it was in Manistique at the time. I did purchase Walthers' mural Docks backdrop and cut out the sky and pasted the building portion of the backdrop to my background between Manistique Pulp & Paper Co. and the carferry. This does fill out that industry and makes it look like the large industry it was. Also, it was on the river and the backdrop was a river scene. I painted some birch trees between the Docks backdrop and the carferry and painted a blue Lake Michigan behind the carferry. Using white paint, I painted clouds in the sky along the entire mural.

Much to my surprise I found doing the background scenery to be a lot of fun. I never thought I would do it myself and never imagined it would be so much fun. It gets the job done of creating an illusion of depth to the railroad and was much more gratifying than just using commercial backdrops and at one-fifth the cost.

Next on the list of things to do with the model railroad was painting and ballasting the track and ground cover. As you know, ties and rail in real life do not look like Atlas flex-track. The ties are not black and the rails are rusted dark brown except for the top. I painted all my ties and rails roof brown though everyone has their own preference on colors and whether the rail and ties should be painted the same color. I just slopped the paint on with a brush and after I did three feet or so I took the paint off the top of the rail with a "bright boy." Along the way I did some deferred maintenance: I replaced ties where I cut ties off to connect track, I put in turnouts where I may someday have new sidings or interchange tracks and I added Tomar bumping posts or wheel stops at the end of sidings. It is best to have the layout in final form trackage-wise before ballasting the track.

I used Woodlands Scenic ballast, a medium gray medium mix for the mainline and a light gray small mix for sidings. I quickly learned that it is easy to put too much ballast on the track and this caused problems when done as it interfered with the wheels of the cars running over the track. I sprinkled a stream of ballast along the middle of the track for three feet or so then, with a wide squared-off paintbrush, pushed it along so it would overflow off to the side of the rails and cover the ends of the ties. I would do this until it was off the top of the ties both between the rails and on the sides. I figured the M&LS mainline was never too well ballasted and my model railroad of it was probably better ballasted than the real railroad ever was.

After pouring the ballast for a length of track I would spray it with water containing just a drop of Palmolive soap from a spray bottle and get the ballast good and wet. Then using a plastic mustard bottle I poured out a stream of Elmer's white glue diluted 50/50 with water and a drop of Palmolive soap between the rails and along either sides.

With the ballast pre-soaked, the glue is sucked right in and within 24-hours the ballast was glued together as hard as rock. When dry I went back and sprinkled with my thumb and index finger a little Woodlands Scenic iron ore down the middle and along either side of the mainline from Doty to the carferry and in Manistique Yard to simulate a seepage of iron ore from the unit ore train movements over the railroad. I then sprayed the track again with water and added the diluted glue and let dry. You must be very careful ballasting the turnouts so they do not get glued shut by the hardened ballast in the points and in the frogs. A polishing of all rails with a bright boy is required afterwards to take ballast and glue off the track.

The next and, unbelievably, last project to complete the railroad was detailing all the industries, buildings, sidings and open areas on the railroad. I was originally going to put in roadways and ground cover first but decided that a lot of this must be done in conjunction with the buildings so I decided to do it on a building-by-building or section-by-section basis instead. Each industry, siding or building needs roads going to it as well as parking lots, weeds and trees, etc. Each one needs piles of the cargo the industry ships or receives lying around the loading docks as well as people working, machinery, cars and trucks. I am currently taking one industry at a time and super-detailing it appropriately. When I do all the Manistique industries I will work on the sidings outside of town and the mainline scenery in between. I figure that, at best, this will take me about six months to finish. When this project is done I will have finished the model railroad. Finished? Is a model railroad ever finished? No, but by "finished" I mean that I will not begin any expansion of the railroad until this last project is done. At this point someone can come down into the basement and see an operating, detailed, scenic'ed, complete model railroad, one that if I never do another thing to will still be completed.

Well, this just about finishes my description of building a model railroad in HO scale. It has been a lot of fun and I am sure will continue to be a lot of fun. The key for me has been keeping the model railroad small and manageable and always building with an eye for future expansion projects so I can incorporate what I have done into other layouts.

November 12, 1991

Dear Editor,

Just thought that I would give you an update on my adventures on modeling the Manistique & Lake Superior Railroad, especially since there are some new twists inspired by you.

I currently have four locomotives assigned to the railroad though I can only operate three at a time. After the Annual Meeting of the AAT&HA this August, I was so Ann Arbor-inspired that I painted up two RS-1s in the Ann Arbor paint scheme. They are not perfect but they are pretty good. I still have to build the frogeye light for the front ends but I decided that something like that is not worth holding me up. Of course, I used the AAT&HAssoc decals. These replaced the fictional M&LS #2 RS-1 I was operating and to some extent AA #3, the S-2 pretending to be an S-1, which is still in the engine house and used to switch the Manistique industrial area.

The blue, gray and white RS-1s are striking and were well worth the work. Since M&LS has the historical precedent of both of them working on the line at one time (albeit in the 1960's instead of the 1950's) I took your advice that it would be more accurate to have one or more of these on the railroad instead of fictitious #2.

For years I owned two brass CN 0-6-0s that I just loved but could not find a place for in any of my modeling dreams. I sold one to a GTW modeler earlier this year but he was not interested in buying the second so it continued to sit in my basement. Then the other day I got the idea that Manistique Pulp and Paper always had its own switcher locomotive, a Whitcomb diesel industrial switch locomotive, and an 0-6-0 steam locomotive is a classic industrial switch engine in the steam days. So why not give MP&P its own switcher on my model railroad and make it the steamer? It works just great. A M&LS north industrial switch job now, instead of switching MP&P as well as the other industries on that spur, sets off cars on the old team track, which is now the MP&P interchange track, and picks up the cars left there by the MP&P crew. The steamer is used to switch the plant before the M&LS engine comes, setting off its pickups on the interchange track, and later, after the new sets-offs are made by the M&LS crew, switches the plant setting off the new cars. If there are more than five cars for MP&P, the MP&P crew and engine come into Manistique Yard to make the swap.

This not only allowed me to get a steam engine on the railroad without stretching the imagination but throws in a new operating twist. We had our first operating session with the MP&P engine last night and it worked great until we had some operating problems with the steamer late in the evening. When that happened we reverted back to the old way where M&LS engine and crew switched MP&P Co. Hopefully the steamer will be in working condition in time for the operating session next month.

The last six months or so have been devoted to fine-tuning the railroad. I have, as mentioned, painted up two Ann Arbor RS-1s and put them on the layout. I got back to my kit-bashed Ann Arbor steel caboose and finished some detail work and decaled and weathered it (I never could find any M&LS caboose decals as Overland was out of them, so I used the Harold King ones and decaled it as an Ann Arbor caboose). I put two tractor/trailers around the industries using Walthers' trailers (one Soo Line). Mostly I have been trying to make the trains run better by working on rough track areas and rolling stock.

I isolated one of my biggest derailment problems to Walthers freight cars, specifically the Walthers' 40' gondolas and 36' tank cars, both of which I have a lot of. It turns out that the Walthers wheels are not made of Delron that

Athearn and MDC use and are thus are more slippery and, on my tight radius curves and #4 turnouts, they are more prone to jump the track. I went to a flea market and bought quite a number of Athearn trucks and replaced all the Walthers and old Train Miniature trucks with them and that solved most of my derailment problems. The Delron wheels of Athearn seem to bite the rail better and thus stay on better. The only problem was that the Athearn trucks did not clear the frame of the Walthers gondola so I kept the Walthers side frames and just replace the wheel sets with Athearn's on those cars. The new trucks worked just swell on the tank cars. The old Train Miniature boxcars wobble with the Athearn trucks but a couple of Kadee red washers seemed to fix that.

January 22, 1992

Dear Editor,

I have been busy on the M&LS model railroad these past two months. I was getting too hung up on the physical logistics of building an Elberta boat yard and carferry so I put that on the back burner and, instead, decided to pursue my other expansion plans of building a hidden interchange yard for the DSS&A and LS&I interchange in the other room of the basement.

I had already put in two turnouts for these interchanges and, over the holidays, I cut two holes into the walls and built a 15-foot by 16-inch bench in the other room. I received an electric screwdriver for Christmas and that, combined with the self-tapping wood screws, is one of man's greatest inventions. I was able to do this new benchwork in one day versus about a week without the electric screwdriver. I did it the right way this time too, with particleboard and higher quality 1" X 3" wood for the frame.

What I plan to build are two, three-track holding yards next to each other back there, one for DSS&A and one for LS&I. Both yards will share a lead track but have their own tracks that actually connect with M&LS. I will eventually have a DSS&A engine (a Baldwin AS-616) and an LS&I engine (an Alco RS-3) painted to do the interchange work. At the beginning of each session and, if the five cars on the interchange tracks in the main train room on the M&LS have turned over, during the session, a crew will use the interchanging railroad's engine and pull the next cut of cars out of the hidden yard and swap them for the cars on the interchange track. In addition, I am going to have three eight-car sets of LS&I ore jennies. Whenever an empty set comes off the boat an M&LS train will take it to the LS&I interchange track and swap it for the loaded ore train already there. After the M&LS train leaves for Manistique, an LS&I train will bring a cut of loaded ore cars from the other room and swap them for the empties on the interchange track.

This new interchange yard will be able to hold five cars on each track, my maximum train size and the number of cars that the interchange tracks can hold. This means five of the six yard tracks will hold a total of 25 general freight cars and one of the LS&I tracks will always have an ore train of eight cars. In addition, the current LS&I interchange was a two-track stub yard at the end of the layout with one track now always empty for the switching. The new LS&I connector track going through the wall can now be used for switching so I can put the third ore train set into the now-empty second interchange track. A total of 41 cars, 25 general freight and 16 ore cars, will be added to the railroad this way, all hidden from view in the main room.

I also plan on adding a fourth throttle for operating the interchange yard. Eventually I will add rotary switches to the control board so that I can run any of the four throttles on any block at any time. I will also add throttle plugs so that the throttles are not tethered to one spot but can be plugged in closer to where you are working with a train.

I have decided to use a cork roadbed for the new section. I am not planning on ballasting it or adding scenery to it at this time as it is hidden from general view. The new yard can be extended another six feet or so should I ever expand the railroad and want to make this into a major yard.

I am currently building the new cars for the expansion. In addition to the sixteen LS&I ore cars, I am adding nine box cars (four of which are Ann Arbor), four coal hoppers, four gondolas (currently all gondolas have pulp wood but when I expand about a third of them will have scrap loads), two reefers, two covered hoppers, two tank cars and two flats.

May 11, 1992

Dear Editor,

   Just thought I would drop you a line about some modeler's information that I have come across lately.

   I ordered, but have not yet received, the Smokey Valley Alco S-1/S-3 replacement hoods for the Atlas switchers you wrote about. I will let you know how they are when they come in.

   The Soo Line Historical and Technical Society DSS&A Division came out with decals for DSS&A's Baldwin AS-616 and Alco RS-1 locomotives. I decaled up a Stewart AS-616 with them and it looks great working the DSS&A interchange on the M&LS at Shingleton. Now all I need is for someone to come out with decals for an LS&I diesel (I am not holding my breath though I dropped the hint to the DSS&A Division).

   I made a slight change to my Soo Line interchange on the M&LS. I switched the old, short interchange track with a long industrial spur leading to one small industry to make the interchange track much longer. I increased the size of the interchange from three cars to five and added a Soo Line AS-16 locomotive and caboose. Now, when five cars are collected for the Soo, the Soo Line train comes into the yard and makes the transfer. The waiting Soo Line interchange train is hidden by trees when buried in the interchange track.

The model railroad continues to be a real joy. The expansion in the other room for the DSS&A and LS&I interchange is working out real well though it is not a full time job for a crew. The rest of the year is going to be spent detailing things like cabooses for all the railroad, the locomotives, etc. as well as adding the pulpwood cars and switching all the toggles switches to rotaries on the control panel. My next expansion plans are to add a boat yard and carferry as well as a couple more industries but these I am putting off until next year.

As an introduction to the next letter to the editor, I succumbed to the wishes of my three young children and decided to build them an HO Scale model railroad that they can operate. As you will see, this eventually evolved into a major expansion of my model railroad, what we can refer to as Phase Two of it. More of this in the next chapter.

May 21, 1993

Dear Editor,

I haven't written in a while and thought that I'd do so and update you on my M&LS model railroad layout.

I spent the entire winter building an 8 X 10 layout for my children so there has been no major building projects on the M&LS since I last wrote you about the DSS&A and LS&I interchange expansion in the winter of 1992. However, there have been a lot of operational changes in the past year.

Though the physical dimensions of the railroad did not grow in the past year, the number of freight cars on the railroad did. I was up to almost 200 cars at one point. This worked well as long as I operated on the system that you switch one for one, meaning if you have one car waybilled for an industry or interchange, you took one car out of that interchange or industry. Likewise, we never did an interchange pull for the LS&I, DSS&A or the Soo Line until five cars were destined for that railroad. The railroad operated quite well this way for over two years and allowed for a maximum number of cars on the layout.

Also, all trains were limited to five cars maximum because of siding lengths. This often resulted in two trains "on the road" to Shingleton and Doty at a time as Manistique yard was generating more cars going north than it could handle. This way there could be meets in the sidings without any problems.

The first big operational change came last year when I decided not to limit trains to five cars. Suddenly we were getting trains as long as 12 cars on road trains. This was a lot of fun and resulted in the more prototypical one road-train per operating session. Often we had to double-head the two RS-1s to handle the road-trains, especially if there was a cut of iron ore coming out of Doty. I purchased for future use a set of the Alco FA-2 "covered wagon" locomotives in Alco demonstrator colors last year. For one operating session we even said that the M&LS was deadheading the Alco demonstrator FA-2 A-B-A set from the Soo Line to DSS&A for demonstrating on the DSS&A. As the trains were so long lately the extra power was a help. When the DSS&A came looking for the demonstrators we said that we lost them and couldn't find them on the railroad but we are looking and switched all our operations to night time so we could use them. One night DSS&A's Pinkerton men were waiting at Shingleton and seized the locomotives so we had to send an RS-1 up from Manistique to finish the run.

The next big operational change came last month when I decided to abandon the one-for-one switching approach. Now, each industry or siding has a "hold" and "pickup" divider in the card pocket. If you are assigned to switch the Manistique industries you will pull all cars for all industries that are in the "pickup" side of the pocket. Sometimes you will have no cars to pick up from an industry (they aren't loaded/unloaded yet), sometimes all the cars. Sometimes, when you complete your pulls, you may only have a couple cars. Sometimes many. Then you deliver your set-offs as they are waybilled. Sometimes some industries may be without cars, sometimes too many cars for their siding. All in all, a more prototypical operation. Likewise on the road trains: You may have a pickup at Hiawatha or Steuben siding even though you do not have a car going to it. With the interchanges, you picked up whatever cars are there regardless of the number (if any) cars in your train going to that interchanging railroad. This removed the artificial controls I had built into the operating sessions and made it as close as possible to the operations of a real railroad.

The end result of this has been the removal of 40 cars from the railroad. Since the traffic flow is not controlled, Manistique yard could too easily become swamped if nothing much went out on a train but 20 cars came back. Removing 40 cars has made the flow smoother. I picked 1953 as the date of my railroad and removed all cars built or carrying paint schemes newer than that as well as all of the old wooden double-sheathed cars without dreadnought ends that would not be running in 1953. All the iron ore cars are gone.

One of my ideas in modeling M&LS was that it would be fun to someday have a steam railroad. Just like you could model the M&LS with one Alco switcher, so could you model it with one light 2-8-0 steam locomotive. This thought was rekindled with my picking the date of 1953. I researched Hugh Hornstein's articles and made note of the style of the steam engines M&LS had in the late 40's and early 50's. Turns out that my local hobby shop had a used Sunset Great Northern light 2-8-0 Consolidation steam locomotive for sale on consignment that was pretty darn close to the steam locomotives that M&LS had.

To make a long story short, I bought the Consolidation steam locomotive and the M&LS is now a steam railroad. For the time being I removed a couple more cars to make the railroad circa 1949 and have been running nothing but the consolidation. For my next operation session, though, the year will have to move back to 1953 and we will run the steamer and diesel together so we have an extra engine. Though I doubt that M&LS ever ran them together, Hugh does not definitively state otherwise, only that "almost" immediately after the diesel arrived the remaining steamers left the property. I will hang my hat on the word "almost."

It would be fun to pick up another 2-8-0, especially a little huskier one more similar to LS&I's 2-8-0s as M&LS did own an ex-LS&I steamer in 1952 and if I ever do a DSS&A layout it can become the LS&I interchange engine.

But, with the price of brass steam engines, even used, it will be a while, if ever, before I even look for one.

I still do not have a carferry built, just a three-track stub with each track representing a carferry load. Tentatively a carferry is on my list as a 1993 project, if not sooner.

That was the last of my many letters to the editor detailing the building of my first model railroad. I am glad I wrote the letters as I was able to catch my ideas and actions in writing shortly after they happened and did not allow time to intervene and take away from the details.

CHAPTER 5

BULDING A MODEL RAILROAD FOR MY CHILDREN AND THE EXPANSION OF MINE

I had accomplished my goal of building and, just as importantly, finishing a model railroad. It took me only about two years to do so but, of course, I did think small and built a good starter one. If I never did anything else I had a fun, working model railroad with the M&LS, one that I could invite a couple friends over to come and operate. And operate it we did. I tried to have an operating session once a month.

Of course, you never really finish building a model railroad until you tear it down and that has proven to be the case with mine. Even when it was done I was constantly fine-tuning the operations or tweaking a portion of the layout, usually with the hidden agenda of trying to get more freight cars on the layout. I quickly found out that the reason for most layout expansions was that you want to get more freight cars on the layout that you purchased and want to see run. It is very hard to take freight cars off the model railroad for some reason and you always want and need more.

I was very surprised at how much work and how expensive it was to detail the model railroad with non-railroad items such as motor vehicles, people figures, trees, crates, etc. This is a whole industry in itself. I was amazed at all the time and money I spent on this aspect of my model railroad. But it really adds a lot to the final product and is a very fun part of the hobby.

My wife, Elaine, though she knew my intentions from the get-go of having a model railroad that I would operate with friends, didn't really focus on the fact that I would have people over in our basement to play with my trains until my first operating session. Our basement was not finished. There was no suspended ceiling and, though it did have a carpet, it was old and moldy. I did hang a lot of fluorescent lights down there in between the joists to give us plenty of light to operate but it was all wired together by extension cords and didn't add to the looks of the basement.

I was perfectly content with the basement as it looked. I only saw this beautiful model railroad. However, Elaine was insistent and finally talked me into getting it remodeled. She found someone to put in a suspended ceiling and then she had new carpeting installed. It did make a big difference and I was glad she did it. It also was good timing as the model railroad was still small and there was plenty of open space to work in for the remodeling.

An interesting event on the model railroad in the early years was a trick I pulled on Ned. I deliberately designed the railroad to have all freight cars be a scale 40-foot or smaller size. Thus, all sidings, run-arounds and spurs were of a size that accommodated 40-foot or smaller cars quite well. Everyone knew this too and it fit in well with my 1950's era though it did restrict me somewhat in types of freight cars I ran.

I had purchased but did not have on the railroad at that time two 50' cars. One was a Pere Marquette 50' double door boxcar and the other was a 50' Milwaukee Road flatcar, both stock Athearn items. One day I decided to put them on the railroad but neglected to tell anyone, as it didn't seem any big deal at the time.

In downtown Manistique on the model railroad there was the industrial switch area. An important part of the operation of switching this industrial area was a short run-around track found there that you often needed to use to get your locomotive on the correct side of freight cars you were shoving into industrial sidings. This run-around could handle three 40' cars and no more without fouling the switches, which couldn't be fouled in order for the locomotive to run-around the cars.

At the first operating session after I added the two 50' cars, Ned was assigned to switch the industrial area of Manistique. Being used to there only being 40' cars, Ned was confidently doing his job, one that he had done many times before and had mastered, when suddenly he stopped dead. He couldn't run around his train with three freight cars in the run-around. This just befuddled him. Turns out two of the three cars were the two 50-footers I added. It took him awhile before he suddenly yelled out "where the heck did these cars come from: there aren't supposed to be 50' cars on the railroad!" We all had a good laugh at his misfortune of getting not one but both of these new, longer cars in his train.

I deliberately designed my model railroad so that it was 45 inches off the ground. This is not only a good working height for operating while standing for most people but it also made it too high off the ground for my three young children to reach. Of course, they eventually grew up and could reach it but they were theoretically more agile and responsible when older than they were in 1991.

Little did I know that this 45-inch height would cause problems. The model railroad was an "attractive nuisance" and the kids really wanted to partake in it. They had to stand on a bench in order to be able to see the layout and this wasn't all that satisfactory to them. Plus, the model railroad wasn't made for kids to operate as kids just like seeing trains move and move fast and preferably in circles and liked to touch them. My model railroad had none of these features.

Since my railroad was alongside the wall of a good-sized rectangular room in the basement there was plenty of room in the middle for children things. I decided to go along with my kids' wishes and build them a small model railroad that we could put in the middle of the basement.

I spent a lot of time talking to my three kids about it. They had some good ideas. My goal was two-fold: build a model railroad for them that they could have fun with now and also make sure that it had some growing room so that they could learn about operations instead of just running trains in circles when they grew tired of that.

At this time *Model Railroad Magazine* was running a series of articles on building a beginner's model railroad. It was on a 4 X 8 layout like we were planning and had many of the same ideas I had and a lot of other good ones. For example, it had a tall board running diagonally across the middle so that when on one side of the layout you could not see the other side. It also had an elevated section in the middle to add some depth to the layout instead of it all being flat at one level. The article was also good to show the kids how to follow and get ideas from other's ideas, using the best and adding your ideas to it.

My basic rule, which I never violated, was that the kids had to help me build the entire layout. Not necessarily all three kids at once but at least one kid always had to be with me when I worked on it. This way it was the kids' railroad and they could learn and appreciate all the work it takes as well as maybe develop some skills in the process.

Needless to say, this kid-participation rule made building it much more difficult than had I done so on my own. It was worth it in the end, but I am getting a little ahead of myself again.

Instead of trying to recall and recite all the details about building this model railroad for kids, I wrote an article on this for *Model Railroad Magazine* and am reproducing it here. It was never published in the magazine. Here it is:

I had a problem that I did not think was unique to me. I have a model railroad in HO scale in the basement and I also have three young children. A model railroad attracts the attention of children like nothing else and my children and their friends always wanted to play with my trains. The problem is that my layout is a little too delicate and complicated for children. At least until they are a little older, I have to be there to operate it with the kids to make it work with all the electrical blocks and throttles and switches we adults love but that do not lend themselves to little kids' interests or intellects.

The solution to the problem was to build the kids their own model railroad. Their railroad would be at their height and would be fairly simple to operate. It would also be sophisticated enough so that when they outgrew running trains in circles there would be sidings and industries to switch so they could operate trains like their old man and his friends do on his layout.

The payoff of making the kids' model railroad more than just a circle track is that, with a little bit a thought, it can be easily combined into the adult model railroad when the adults are operating, yet can remain a simple, stand-alone layout when the kids are operating it. That way, all the time and effort you spent in building it can pay off in two ways: a hobby for your children and an expansion to your model railroad.

Lets start at the beginning. In late 1989, I decided to build a model railroad based on an abandoned (since 1968) Michigan Upper Peninsula shortline, the Manistique & Lake Superior Railroad. Since this was my first attempt at model railroading, I purposefully picked a shortline that I had a lot of historical resources to model through the Ann Arbor Technical and Historical Association, as the M&LS was owned by the Ann Arbor Railroad, and that I could model the entire railroad fairly prototypically in a small area. I did not have a lot of money to spend on model railroading, nor did I have any unique skills. I built the railroad on a tight budget and learned every aspect of it as I built it (with a lot of advice from friends who had model railroads). I picked 1953 as the year I was modeling.

The HO M&LS in my basement is basically a U-shaped model railroad running along the three walls of one 20 X 12 foot room of the basement. The benchwork along one of the long walls comes out 18 inches and that is the town of Manistique, Michigan. Manistique is the center of operations of the M&LS where the freight yard, engine house, industries and the Ann Arbor Railroad's Lake Michigan carferry slip was located. The other two walls are the 34 miles (not to scale) mainline of the M&LS from Manistique north to Shingleton and Doty, where it interchanged with the Duluth, South Shore & Atlantic RR and the Lake Superior & Ishpeming RR, respectively. The mainline is located on a six-inch shelf along these two walls and, except for the small town of Steuben in the one corner, is nothing more than a main track and sidings for the interchanges. As you can see, the M&LS takes up very little room in the basement, leaving the entire middle of the room free for other activities. It is a very active little layout and we can keep three operators very busy during a two-hour operating session.

At some point, my three kids had become very interested in the model railroad and wanted to play with it. They were very young and with my layout being at a very adult height of 45 inches, the kids had to stand on stools or boxes to see what was going on. Also, I had five throttles, 29 blocks, six-position rotary switches and a ton of turnouts that just got in the way of the kids having a good time without dear old dad involved as dispatcher, switch tender, section crew, big hook, etc. More often than not, we all got frustrated and just gave up, especially when all three kids wanted to play at once. Also, the kids didn't like the fact that the trains ran point to point and couldn't understand why I didn't connect the two ends to make a circle, something they could relate too.

It was at this point that we decided to build a model railroad for the kids. My son, who was four at the time, was especially interested in doing this. At the same time, *Model Railroader* had just started running their series entitled *Just for Beginners*, which was a perfect starting point for us.

We agreed that this would not just be Dad's project but that one of the kids would have to be helping me every time we built or in anyway did anything on the model railroad. I also decided to follow the MR article pretty closely so show the kid's how you can use resources like MR to get ideas and use them or improve on them to fit your needs and desires.

That open area in the basement sure came in handy as suddenly a 4 X 8 foot model railroad was going up in that space. We kept things simple and budgeted though we didn't cut any corners when it came matters with respect to how well trains ran on the tracks. There is nothing more frustrating to kids than operating problems like derailments. The railroad had to run well so that dear old dad didn't have to be around whenever the kids wanted to run trains. Also, I wanted everything compatible with my layout (Code 100 track, Shinohara turnouts, Kadee couplers, etc.) so that the kids could grow into mine and so that their layout would run well, and, who knows, maybe there was the thought that someday we might be able to somehow combine the two layouts some way.

I presented my initial thoughts on the layout at dinner one evening and let the kids provide their input. When I suggested a simple circle with sidings and spurs and an elevated middle area for a quarry or so, just like the *Just For Beginners* article, my wife, Elaine, gave the first of many practical suggestions: "You don't expect to build a kid's layout that only one kid can run one train at a time, do you?" So much for preconceived notions on a kid's model railroad. The single-track circle suddenly became a double track circle with two crossovers.

Construction began with a 4 X 8 sheet of plywood we

had in the garage and putting it on an old air-hockey table we had in the basement (we were on a budget). We painted it dark brown just in case we needed that color for scenery purposes. It wasn't attached to the air hockey table so we could move it and play air hockey still. We bought Atlas flex-track and Shinohara turnouts for the layout. I had used cork under the track on parts of my layout but keep it cork-colored. The kids immediately pointed out that the Grand Trunk Western Railroad tracks running behind our house had gray gravel ballast, not brown, so we bought a can of gray spray paint and painted all the cork gray. Then we laid the track.

As mentioned, this was going to be the kids' project and I stuck to that the entire time. I never did a minute of work on the layout without at least one of the kids helping me. Usually it was my son but my two daughters were very active too and many times we had all three kids downstairs working away. A number of projects I did while the kids watched ("supervised" according to them) such as cutting wood with the electric saw. But many of the other tasks, even screwing together wood with the electric screwdriver, could be handled by the kids with supervision. They helped in all projects from laying track to building buildings to scenery and making mountains out of plaster. It was a great experience for the kids and a great family project when handled this way. But be ready for it to take about five times longer to do simple tasks and have plenty of patience for this is not the easiest or quickest way to build a model railroad. For our purposes, though, it was the best way.

As our plans were progressing, I was continually amazed at the preconceived expectations the kids have of what a model railroad should be like. Rarely did one of my ideas get accepted without some modification. I also found out that the kids couldn't believe that I didn't incorporate many of these things into my "grown-up" model railroad and that they were kind of disappointed in their old man and were intent on setting him straight this time on their model railroad.

For instance, in the mind of a child all model railroads must have, at a minimum, a tunnel, a bridge and a mountain. I was planning on the bridge: We were going to have a girder bridge spanning the mainlines on the elevated lead to an elevated quarry in the center of the layout. I was not planning on a mountain or tunnel, as we just do not have those types of scenic things in Michigan. But, you guessed it, we ended up making a mountain where the *Just For Beginners* article had a lake and running the mainlines through it via a tunnel, solving both the mountain and tunnel issue in one stroke. The kids didn't see a need for a lake and cottage anyway.

The kids also like a lot of "bells and whistles," so to speak, on the layout. In some ways this was literal: "How could you, dad, build another model railroad layout without a road crossing protected by flashing lights and a bell?" the kids wanted to know. Looking through the Walthers catalog, we found such a grade crossing kit and installed it in on the railroad, modifying it so that instead of a passing train activating it the kids could turn it on and off with a button. Installing the grade crossing bell and lights was also a good electronic project for us all.

I quickly learned from the kids operating my model railroad layout that they have trouble rerailing HO scale cars. At all the grade crossings on the model railroad we decided to incorporate the Atlas rerailer track so the kids had at least four locations on the railroad (two grade crossings of the two-track mainline) they can easily rerail a car or put on new cars. It is amazing how that simplified their lives and let them be more independent of dear old dad when they operate their trains.

Deciding on what railroad to model or, alternatively, what to name our model railroad was an easy decision. We had a short-line railroad not far from where we live named Coe Rail that the kids were very familiar with. Coe Rail gives train rides on summer weekends that the kids have taken and we even had my son's fourth birthday on a chartered Coe Rail train. When I suggested that we model Coe Rail all the kids agreed that was a good idea.

Problem was that Coe Rail doesn't have mountains, tunnels, bridges or quarries on its railroad but that didn't bother the kids. Kids do not get hung up on prototypicalness like adults do. Modeling Coe Rail turned out to be a good decision as we had a prototype to visit and we also had freight and passenger service plus "birthday specials" to model just like on the real railroad.

We tried to pick out industries for the model railroad that had relevance to the kids. Coe Rail switched a lumberyard and the kids know all about lumberyards. So we purchased the easiest and least expensive lumberyard we could find in HO scale, the one produced by Atlas.

Coe Rail also switched a plastic toy manufacturing company. Talk about a perfect industry to model on a kid's layout! We used a model of a two-stall engine house for the toy factory and run freight cars of all types into it to bring in raw materials and ship out finished toys from the toy factory. It worked out great as almost any type of freight car can be seen there.

Once on a vacation we stopped to see a cement company located on a railroad. The kids were interested in modeling that so we purchased the Faller cement company and put it on a siding on the layout, running covered hoppers into it. When we saw the real cement factory it had old Ann Arbor Railroad and Detroit & Mackinac Railroad covered hoppers on lease to deliver the cement. We purchased the identical Ann Arbor cars from Roundhouse and decaled up the identical Detroit & Mackinac cars using Walthers decals and Roundhouse covered hoppers. It brought home the fun of modeling the prototype to the kids. Though Coe Rail doesn't service a cement plant, there is one on line that it theoretically could.

I purchased a number of Athearn pickle cars for my layout and the kids found it very interesting that pickle cars existed and moved pickles in those big vats on flat cars. We purchased the Model Power Heinz pickle factory and built it and put it on the layout. No such prototype on Coe Rail, but who cares?

Lastly, we had the quarry to model. We expanded our quarry from what *Just For Beginners* did on their layout. We purchased Walthers' Cornerstone Series Red River Mining building and incorporated that into our quarry on the upper level. We decided that, even though a gravel quarry was prototypical in Michigan and could even be found somewhere on Coe Rail, a coal mine would be more fun. So Coe Rail in HO now services a coal mine in the middle of Michigan.

Electrically we tried to keep the layout as simple as possible. We have two throttles and use toggles to control which throttle controls which circle, the inner or outer one. This way two kids can run trains at the same time.

I quickly found that, though switching industries and operating the model railroad somewhat prototypically is fun, it can become too structured for kids. First and foremost the kids want to run trains in circles. Added to this is the picking up of freight cars in the sidings to make longer trains. At least at the age they are now switching and operating quasi-prototypically comes only after about an hour of circle running and then only for the older kids.

We wired up the layout so that there is only one block for each circle but the same throttle could control both circles if desired. This made life very simple and the kids could figure this out easily.

All spurs are powered through the turnouts. This also made life easy. However, there is a compromise in this electrical simplicity. Forgetting to normalize a switch when back on the mainline results in the train dying and the cry of "daddy, problems!" coming from the operator. After awhile, though, the kids learn that when a train suddenly stops to go to the next turnout and see if it needs to be thrown back to normal.

We have two crossovers on the layout to allow trains to go between the inner and outer circle. Other than adding the complication of more switches to forget to normalize and to short-circuit the layout, it works out well and is needed to get from the roundhouse to the outer circle.

Wiring up the turntable and roundhouse tracks in a simple way for the kids was a challenge. We decided to have the roundhouse lead track, turntable and engine house tracks all powered from the turnout off the inner circle mainline. We added a toggle so that the power is either directed to the tracks (lead, turntable and stall) or to the turntable motor. The kids just throw the turnout to the roundhouse lead and, when the engine is on the turntable ready for turning, they throw the toggle and control the turntable through their throttle. When the turntable is positioned correctly, they throw the toggle back and run the engine. An Atlas three-position connector panel gives power to each of the three roundhouse stall tracks as desired. We used the Atlas "metered" turntable so there would be no track alignment issues.

We split up the 4 X 8 layout with a two-foot tall piece of masonite backdrop positioned diagonally, splitting the layout in half in the middle of the two-track circle. We used a Walthers' Scenic Horizons as a backdrop on it. This way the kids cannot see the train when it is on the other side of where they are standing, adding to the imagined length of the layout.

Lastly, we added grass, gravel roads, trees, shrubs, people, animals, vehicles, etc. to the layout to decorate it. Unlike grownup layouts, most of the people, vehicles, loads and animals are not static displays to the kids. The figures alternatively ride the locomotives, cabooses and freight cars as well as watch the trains from the sidelines. The animals ride too, mostly in the stock cars. The gravel/coal hoppers loads are removed when delivered and are later replaced in the cars as are the lumber loads ("can't have an empty freight car have a load in it you know, dad"). In many ways, this is where the kids have the most fun operating the trains.

Rolling stock on the kids' layout is a mixture of various equipment, some surplus cars from my layout, some older era equipment, some modern. Originally we kept with the lock-horn couplers that came with the cars but later replaced them all at one fell swoop with Kadee No. 5 couplers to improve operations. We even have some passenger equipment as the kids love to run passenger trains on the layout. Again, the kids know what they like and they usually like bells and whistles and freight cars they have seen and can relate to. We also make sure we have cars to fit the industries on the layout like pickle cars, coal hoppers, covered hoppers, etc.

Each kid has a locomotive they call their own and there are always some extra locomotives in the box or from my layout. We did paint up one Alco switcher and a caboose in a Coe Rail paint scheme.

We tried a card system for operations basing it on pictures drawn by the kids instead of writing because the younger two kids couldn't read yet. I found that they rarely used it as it was too structured for young kids and they rather just play with the trains than operate them prototypically.

After building the kids' layout over one winter, we had it completed as we had originally planned. It has provided the kids with two years of enjoyment and was a great family project.

After about a year, the kids starting making noises about how nice it would be if their model railroad layout could be somehow connected to mine. I pointed out that mine was too high off the ground for them and, anyway, I wasn't about to completely change the geography of my railroad to somehow incorporate theirs. In reality, I didn't know if I wanted to share. The main reason for building the kids' layout was so that they would not operate mine.

But also at this time the cold weather was coming back for another winter and I was getting the bug to work on the model railroad. Building the kids' layout satisfied this urge to build last year but what about this coming winter?

Then the thought occurred to me. Why couldn't we keep the kids' layout at a lower level and have a connecting ramp between their layout and mine. I ran this by my model railroad friends one day at lunch and they pointed out that my Soo Line interchange on the M&LS really wasn't modeled in such a way to be as important an interchange as it was on the real M&LS. Why not, they suggested, make the kids' layout the Soo Line Railroad at Manistique, with its own tracks, yard and industries to switch and have the interchange track between the two railroads on a long connecting ramp that bridges the height difference.

This was the kernel of rationale I was looking for. The kids' model railroad was a first-class layout that took a year of work. Suddenly, with the addition of a connecting ramp,

I had an instant addition to my railroad. And, best of all, I had an addition without disrupting the concept of either mine or the kids' model railroad; in fact we added to both layout's concepts by enhancing a weak interchange point on mine and by tapping into my larger layout with the kids'.

The most important part of this merger of the two railroads was to keep them both separate and distinct so that both layouts could be used for their intended purposes but also to enhance both layouts by creating a synergism from the two.

Except for a connecting track, nothing was done to the layout of either of the model railroads. The kids' layout was still a double tracked circle with the same industries. Mine was still a U-shaped point-to-point layout. In fact, all that was added to mine was a turnout just outside of Manistique yard to the connecting track. All we did to the kids' layout was extend the ramp to the coal mine on the elevated level so as to continue the grade into the connecting ramp.

What we did first was anchor the kids' layout to the wall so that it was a permanent island reaching eight feet into the center of the basement from a point centered and below the bottom of the "U" on my U-shaped layout. The next project was building the connecting ramp between the two layouts.

At first I had planned a long, curving ramp to act as the interchange track between the two layouts. However, the height difference and the lack of running room would have made the grade insurmountable.

Don't get me wrong. The gradient of the connecting ramp is not prototypical. It is probably around 10%. It was a big temptation to raise the level of the kids' layout to decrease this grade and it would have been easy to do so since the kid's layout was an unattached, stand-alone layout. But in keeping with the philosophy that the kids have to be able to use their layout, we decided to compromise with the steep grade of the connecting ramp.

The intention was to make the connecting ramp an interchange track and not part of a mainline so the steepness of the grade wasn't all that important. We also never planned on running more that five or so cars a time on the ramp and we could always double-head power or double-the-hill if we needed to. To help the grade, my son Mike had the great idea that we split the ramp into two portions, with a switchback half-way up. This made the grade more manageable. Eventually I decided that for my railroad's operations the interchange would be at the switchback, halfway up the ramp, instead of at the M&LS Yard in Manistique on the upper level, and we put a two-track spur there for the interchange. This way the M&LS interchange train would only have to go halfway down the ramp and, likewise, the Soo Line interchange train would only have to go halfway up the ramp to make the interchange.

The kids liked the connecting ramp not only as access to my model railroad but also just for the fun of running a train up the hill. Right after we first hooked up the ramp and had it wired up, my son took his locomotive out of the lower level engine house, coupled onto a cut of his freight cars and a caboose and ran the train up the ramp and onto my railroad, set-off his cars in my freight yard and coupled onto a cut of my cars and took them back down onto his layout via the connecting ramp. After he had yarded his train and took the engine to the enginehouse, silent the whole time of this move, he looked at me and said, "I have been wanting to do that for a long time, dad." Though the kids do take advantage of the connecting ramp to run their trains on my railroad on occasion, it hasn't been as often as I had thought and never really disrupts my layout all that much, something I was originally concerned with.

Not true the other way around. When I have an operating session, the kids' layout is now an integral part of my operations. It is not only the Soo Line Railroad interchange at Manistique but it is the Soo Line Railroad on the lower level with industries to switch in addition to making the interchange. Usually one person is assigned to Soo Line/Manistique and he is kept busy the entire session there. It truly has been the logical and perfect expansion to my railroad, totally adding to it and not detracting from it in any way.

In order to continue to follow our philosophy of keeping things simple on the kids' layout, we wired up the ramp as simply as possible. Instead of giving it a separate electrical block, the lower half of the ramp is powered by the same turnout that powered it before it was extended. The upper half is powered by the track "block" the turnout to the ramp is located on my railroad. The middle, interchange portion is powered from either source depending on which way a toggle switch is thrown. Toggle down means it is powered from the lower level. Toggle up means it is powered from the upper level. Simple for the kids to remember.

The kids' layout continues to use its isolated, stand-alone electrical power so that it can be operated independent of my layout. When operating it as the Soo Line Railroad during my sessions, the operator just uses the same throttles the kids use when they operate it. Since the interchange is at the middle of the connecting ramp, the Soo Line operator just continues using his lower level throttle, making sure that the toggle to supply power to the interchange portion of the ramp is down so he controls the section of track there. When the M&LS interchange crew comes down the ramp, he uses the same throttle he is using on the upper level to reach the mid-point interchange track, just making sure that the toggle is in the proper position when he gets there so he controls it.

At first blush the idea of a circular layout is not very prototypical to the sophisticated model railroad operator. However, we have found that when we were using the kids' circular layout in our adult operations it worked out just fine. You had to go back and forth between the two circles in order to switch the industries and the yard using the crossovers. As it turned out, the circles are like long (some say perpetual) run-around tracks and, with the backdrop divider inhibiting your view of the other side of the layout, they act more as such than as a circle. The Soo Line Manistique yardmaster usually uses one-half of one of the circles as a yard track so it is tied up with freight cars anyway, thus breaking the circle.

The concept of the kids' layout being modeled after Coe Rail when they are playing with it and transforming into Soo Line when the grownups operate has worked perfectly. I usually remove the two or three Soo Line engines I placed on their layout and put back their engines after my operating sessions and, except for different freight cars being on their layout after my session, things revert to normal. Many times the kids run a locomotive from my engine house down the ramp to their layout and use that for their session and that is fine. I usually give them free rein with however they want to operate but I do have to go over all the cars before my session to make sure everything is where it was when we left it. Usually it is not and I just take the time to put all the cars back where their waybills say there are. Recently I have made the cleanup a semi-structured operating session for the kids where they are using locomotives and trains to set-off all the freight cars where they belong on both railroads so I can be ready for my session. This is a fun way to "pick up," something all kids usually hate to do with their toys.

One unmentioned reason I didn't raise the level of the kids' layout when connecting it to mine was that their level was the perfect height to entirely clear all the benchwork underneath my model railroad. I knew that as ingenious the connecting ramp was, the kids would want longer train runs at some point and I would again get the urge to expand and build a model railroad, as happened as described below.

Phase Three was when we decided later that year to take the concept of modeling the Soo Line Railroad one step further and build an entire separate railroad underneath mine, using the kids' layout as part of it. What we did was expand the Soo Line Railroad from just being in the City of Manistique to the entire First Division of the old Soo Line Railroad running from Sault Ste Marie, Michigan through Manistique to Gladstone, Michigan, a division point and the location of a large freight yard in Michigan's Upper Peninsula. How we did this was easy. We already had the kids' layout anchored to the wall at the lower level. We merely added benchwork underneath my original U-shaped layout at the same level connecting into the kids' circle.

Now the kids' layout can still be a stand-alone kid's circular layout or it can be part of a larger lower-level end-to-end layout. The interchange with the M&LS via the connecting ramp is still there and is still used the same way. However, for my operating session, the lower level is a separate, large operating layout, connecting with the M&LS at the upper level by the interchange of cars just like the prototype. The lower level has classification yards at each end (Sault Ste. Marie and Gladstone) with the major city containing industries being Manistique at the kids' layout in the island which all Soo Line trains pass through.

Electrically, we now incorporated the wiring of the upper level into the lower level with the lower level having its own control panel showing all the electrical blocks located on the lower level. Four of the eight throttles are common to both levels with the upper level having two "yard' throttles unique to that level and the lower level having one throttle unique to its level and one "yard" throttle only controlling the kids' layout.

Five different throttles can operate the entire lower level, including the kids' layout. The inner circle and the outer circle of the kids' layout are two separate blocks on the control panel for the lower level, the same concept as we originally wired it for. The kids' layout has two throttles that are fed by their own power source so they do not have to turn on my layout to operate theirs. One of the two throttles are part of the entire lower level block system and is a position on the lower level control panel rotary switches. The other only operates the kids' layout circles and is accessed by a toggle for the inner and outer circle that overrides the control panel. Again, we tried to keep the kids' layout as separate and simple as possible electronically for their ease of use. At the same time it introduced them to my block system and how that is controlled and operated and also being able to incorporate their layout into my block system for the entire layout.

Currently when I have an operating session the entire lower level, including the kids' layout, is operated as a separate railroad by its own "Soo Line Crews" and the original upper level is likewise operated with its own "M&LS Crews." The only interface between the railroads and the two levels is the interchange of cars between the two in a prototypical fashion via the connecting ramp between the two levels. We run road trains between Sault Ste. Marie and Gladstone with pickups and setoffs at Manistique. Crews are assigned to each of these three lower level locations.

I wanted to avoid having two separate waybill systems for each level but my big concern was that I would have too many cars operating between the two levels at one time via the upper and lower level Soo Line/M&LS interchange or, worse yet, the flow of cars always being one way, either up or down, between the two levels. I got lucky because two of the four interchanges on the M&LS layout, the Duluth, South Shore & Atlantic Railroad and the Lake Superior & Ishpeming Railroad ones, are also interchanges on the Soo Line First Division. Soo Line interchanged with DSS&A at Sault Ste. Marie and at Trout Lake on the Soo Line First Division and with the LS&I at Eben Junction on the Rapid River Branch Line. I incorporated the Trout Lake interchange with the DSS&A and the Rapid River Branch Line ending at the interchange with LS&I on the lower level. This way any car with a destination to DSS&A or LS&I doesn't have to automatically go to the upper level from the lower level but, instead, stays on the lower level and is interchanged with those railroads there. This along with the creating of many new waybills and empty/return to library pocket cards with destinations on the lower level has kept the flow of cars between levels at the M&LS/Soo Line interchange pretty even. Best of all, I can just keep the one pool of waybills for use regardless of what level you are working on instead of having two separate ones, one for each level, and trying to keep track of them.

The best thing about my two-level model railroad, next to the fact that the kids still have their own railroad and that I am able to incorporate it into my operating sessions, is that I am able to model two separate railroads. I was able to keep my beloved Manistique & Lake Superior shortline on the upper level yet separately model and operate a larger, more mainline railroad that I have always wanted to model, Soo Line, on the lower level. Emotionally, I am not yet ready to abandon the M&LS: it was my first railroad and I still enjoy it. This plus the fact that a lot of hard work went into it and I just couldn't change it so fast, at least not yet.

However, the more I model the Soo Line on the lower level, the more attached I am to it. I can see the emotional interest shifting away from M&LS to Soo Line the longer I model Soo Line.

From the above article you can see what happened next with my model railroad. As I said, a model railroad is never done.

The addition of the kids' layout to mine as the first phase of my expansion was very interesting. The idea of having it be a second railroad (the Soo Line) in Manistique, a small town that did have these two railroads was a pretty unique idea. However, I do not think that the concept sunk in very well with my operators. They had a hard time conceptualizing it and, though they could operate it, they would have had a better time if they had understood the geography better. The problem was that none of them were familiar with the real town of Manistique and the lay of the land, so to speak.

The resulting grades between the two levels were steep, but manageable. Heck, we were only moving five cars maximum a time up the grade for the interchange anyway. We did have some wild run-aways, though, on this interchange but it served a purpose and worked out fine for the time. It avoided a lot of other problems and let me connect the two levels.

It was fun to model the Soo Line even though it was in a small capacity. I had purchased a Stewart Baldwin AS-16 painted as Soo Line from a friend as a locomotive at one time for the original, short Soo Line interchange on the upper level and started using this as the local switcher on the lower level. This locomotive wasn't heavy or powerful enough to shove five cars up the grade to the interchange so I added two Walthers Fairbanks-Morse switchers painted in Soo Line when they came out. One could handle the grade but we often ran them both together.

I really struggled with the idea of expanding the lower level beyond the kids' island layout. It was not the correct way to build a model railroad: starting out with the top level then building a lower one underneath it. But after thinking about it and surveying it out I decided I could do it and that it may work out rather well. Suddenly the lower level became the larger model railroad and the original upper level the smaller.

I decided to continue modeling the Soo Line on the lower level, as I really liked the Soo Line. I bought all sorts of locomotives for Soo Line, including FA-1s that E-M Enterprises imported from Brazil painted in the maroon

Soo Line scheme for road power. I decaled up some RS-1s for yard power and got some more AS-16s that I decaled for Soo Line. Pretty soon I had too much Soo Line power.

I also decided to run passenger trains on the Soo Line. They ran passenger trains on this line in the 1950's and I always wanted to have a passenger train operation on a model railroad probably because all the fun we had with them on Bill's E&M layout. I bought a lot of Roundhouse Harriman-type cars painted for Canadian Pacific Railway and redid the lettering on them for Soo Line. I had two passenger trains on the line, each with their own locomotives. One had two of the beautiful Atlas FP-7s painted in the Soo Line maroon paint scheme. The other had two Atlas GP-7s that I painted and decaled for Soo Line, even adding the relocated air tank "torpedo tubes" to their roofs to make them passenger geeps. We ran one each way every operating session and boy did they look good.

I had a lot of fun running all sorts of locomotive on Soo

Line made by all sorts of model railroad manufacturers. This gave me an opportunity to try out all different ones and also have a lot of variety of locomotive types. The best running ones were the Stewart F-3s I had. The Atlas FP-7s and Atlas GP-7s were very nice runners. The two Walthers' F-M switchers were superb and were very heavy so they were great pullers up the connecting ramp. The Atlas RS-1 was also great. The Stewart AS-16s were good when I repowered them with the Kato chassis that Stewart came out with in a second run. The only problem was that even with the extra body weights that came with the Kato chassis they still were too light and were not good pullers, which was contrary to Baldwin's reputation. I also had a set of Athearn F-7s and Bachman Spectrum F-7s to try out less expensive locomotive models on the railroad. These ran OK but you could not compare them to the other manufacturers. Same with the E-M Enterprise FA-1s. These looked good and ran adequately but were not up the standards of the more expensive ones. The Spectrum, Athearn and E-M were half the price, though.

CHAPTER 6

MODELING THE ANN ARBOR RAILROAD

The next phase of my model railroad happened out of coincidence. Bill had suspended operations on his model railroad as he was retiring and moving into a condo. In this interlude the thought occurred to me that it might be fun to "borrow" his model carferry and somehow incorporate it into my model railroad.

I had always wanted to model the Ann Arbor Railroad. It was a fun Michigan railroad that I was able to railfan some before it went out of business in the early 1980's. Bill's now unused carferry would be a perfect solution to my dilemma of connecting the upper and lower levels of the model railroad. My plan was a stroke of genius.

The Ann Arbor Railroad operated a carferry across Lake Michigan from Elberta, Michigan. Its northern half, from Owosso, in the middle of the State, to its Boat Yard and carferry slip in Elberta, was a division of the railroad. The clincher was that the AA owned the M&LS and even sailed a carferry to it in Manistique! And now I had a model of a carferry and a very good one at that. This was meant to be.

The timing was also perfect. Up to this point it was very hard to model the AA as none of its all-Alco post-steam motive power was available in plastic HO Scale models. Now Atlas had their Alco S-2/S-4 diesel switcher, which, with a change of hoods to make it an S-1 or S-3 model that was made by another model railroad company, worked fine. Ann Arbor had eight of these switchers. Atlas had their RS-1 roadswitcher out now, of which AA had two of. And just at this time Proto 2000 was coming out with an ALCO FA-2 road locomotive in an Ann Arbor Railroad painted version. Whereas a couple years earlier you wouldn't have considered modeling the AA as you could never model its first-generation diesels, now you had no reason not to as they were all available. And the Ann Arbor Railroad historical society produced decals for the switchers and the RS-1s.

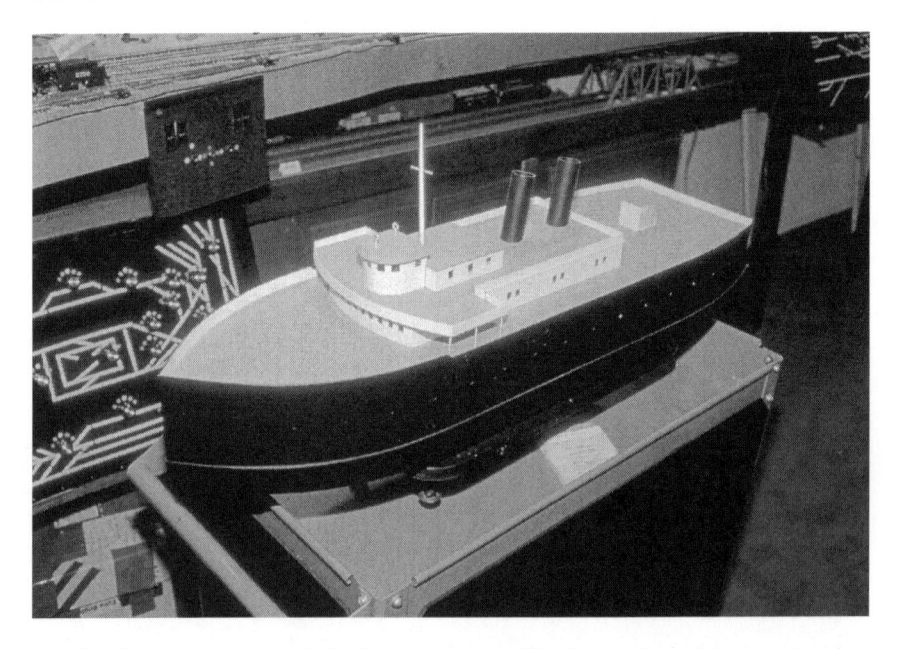

I had already modeled their two RS-1s and was running them as leased power on the M&LS, which had a historical precedent. I started painting up and decaling eight of the simple black and white switchers and purchased eight FA-2s and I thus had the entire AA locomotive roster, less their 44-ton Whitcomb industrial switcher, which I eventually did using a Spectrum GE 44-tonner.

Next I had to modify the lower level of the layout to

become the Ann Arbor Railroad instead of the Soo Line. This was easy to do as. Without any structural benchwork changes I converted it into an Owosso to Elberta route. The one end, which was Sault Ste. Marie on the Soo Line layout, became Owosso. The kids' island in the middle became the City of Cadillac and included an interchange with the Pennsylvania Railroad that once was the DSS&A interchange on the prior model railroad. The other end was Elberta Boat Yard. The old LS&I Eben Jct. interchange branchline became the C&O Railroad line from Traverse City and Boardman Yard to Thompsonville for the C&O interchange there.

I had to redo all the waybills to make routings work for the new lower level but that wasn't too hard. I also had to rename the industries in what was now Cadillac to fit industries existing in Cadillac at that time. I also made some new industries there. Cadillac, as it was before with Manistique on the lower level, was the only town with industries on the lower level layout.

I was able to find an article in the Ann Arbor Railroad Technical & Historical Association newsletter about what industries existed in Cadillac in the 1950's that the Ann Arbor RR serviced. I also took a trip to Cadillac around this time and kicked around town a little to see what was still there. I used this as a basis to either convert my existing industries on the lower level in what was now going to be Cadillac to proper, historic industries or to build some new industries there. This was a lot of fun researching and doing. On the elevated level in Cadillac, where there was once Inland Lime & Stone and its quarry for the Soo Line layout, I changed it to Malleable Iron and bought a building from the Walthers' Cornerstone Steel

Mill series and kit-bashed it for this. I also bought the Walthers' Cornerstone furniture building and built it for St. John's Furniture in Cadillac. Later, when Bill dismantled his railroad, I bought his Cadillac Brick Company and all the associated clay ovens and put it on the site of the old quarry on the middle level, another classic Cadillac industry.

The only benchwork modifications/expansions I had to do to accommodate the carferry was that I needed a carferry slip at both Manistique on the upper level and Elberta Yard on the lower level. This was fairly easy to do as I had room in the aisle at both locations to extend the benchwork out a little. I put in a triangular expansion in both areas at the end of the benchwork. In both locations I did add track to the yards there (in the case of Manistique I made a yard into what had been a long industrial spur by adding two tracks). The tricky job was the three turnouts required for the carferry slip itself to go from one lead track to the carferry's four-track deck. I used a #6 wye for the first split then cut two #6 turnouts for the next splits, making sure I cut them so that they matched the other ends of the turnouts that were part of the carferry deck.

The slip itself was difficult to make to match the carferry's attachment mechanism. It wasn't perfect and you had to hand-maneuver the carferry once it was docked and locked into place to make sure the tracks were lined up. Otherwise, I copied the docking mechanism exactly like Bill's.

Another issue was how to get the carferry to elevate from one level to the other. Bill's carferry slips were at the same level so the carferry's height was stationary. He had it on top of an office cart on wheels so he could "sail" it across the room by pushing it. I needed to sail it but also raise and lower it.

What I did was take a plastic pipe and punched a hole through the middle of the metal table, anchoring it to the floor of the table. I then took a smaller diameter metal pipe that fit inside the first and connected this one to the wooden plank that the carferry rested on. I measured the pipes so that, when in the down position completely, the carferry was at the correct height for the lower level. Then I cut a hole into the outside pipe so that when the carferry was in the upper position for the upper level the inside pipe cleared this hole and, by inserting a bolt through it, when you lowered the carferry to where the inside pipe rested on the bolt the carferry was at the correct upper level height. When the bolt was removed and the carferry was lowered all the way it could go it was at the correct height for docking at the lower level slip.

This "sea-locks" method of operating the carferry was one of my few engineering moments of genius and it worked just great. It was a unique way to connect two levels of a model railroad without steep grades or a double helix. Once I had someone new over to the layout, a mechanical engineer, and when he saw how the carferry worked and how it fit into the model railroad he said it was very "clever."

Within a very short period of time the Ann Arbor Railroad was in business. Not before, however, I had my "last run" of the Soo Line lower level. I invited everyone over to a regularly scheduled operating session that I did not advertise as the last run as no one knew my plans to convert to the Ann Arbor RR at the time. I videotaped much of the evening. I really enjoyed modeling the Soo Line and still miss it. However, I was changing it to a railroad I liked even more, the Ann Arbor Railroad.

The first run of the Ann Arbor Railroad worked out real well. The first thing that struck me was that the operators picked up the new operations very quickly. When I later pointed this out and asked why, the response was that they knew the Ann Arbor Railroad better than they knew the Soo Line and were familiar with the geography of the Ann Arbor and the Lower Peninsula of Michigan more so than they were of the Soo Line layout based in the Upper Peninsula. I realized that this was key to a good operating railroad: Model something people are familiar with and things will run better.

You must remember that I made the changeover to the Ann Arbor assuming that I only had Bill's carferry for a temporary period of time. What I immediately started once I changed the railroad over to the Ann Arbor was to build my own carferry. I used Bill's as the prototype and tried to duplicate its dimensions as best as possible.

I am not a very good craftsman and I had a difficult time building my own carferry. But it was a lot of fun and I am glad I did it. It by no means looks as good as Bill's (which was built for him by an engineer) but it works just as well and gets the job done. It took me close to a year to build it. The irony of it was that when it was about $2/3^{rds}$ complete Bill decided to sell me his carferry.

Suddenly I had two carferries, or almost two. The question was, should I just stop building mine or complete it? I decided to complete it as it was almost done and I had a lot of enjoyment in the project and wanted to see it to completion. Then the question was what to do with two carferries. After a little thought on the matter I decided I could have both carferries on the model railroad.

Having two carferries meant that there was always one at a dock so both boat yards always had a carferry to load and unload. This also allowed me to have 30 more cars on the railroad (the capacity of two carferries). This was another stroke of genius. Now we have two carferries and usually once an operating session they both sail across Lake Michigan, passing each other, which is always a showstopper.

The modeling of a carferry seems to be pretty uncommon in model railroads. Maybe it is because there were not too many carferry operations in the United States. It certainly was an interesting aspect of Michigan railroading and was fun to incorporate it in a model railroad. It is fascinating to watch someone switching the carferry and pulling out more and more freight cars from it.

Some of the operators take switching the carferry very seriously. They know how the carferries had to be switched in real life and try to duplicate it. Since the freight cars made the carferries top heavy it was necessary never to switch out or in freight cars so that there were too many on any one side of the ship at one time. Because of this, you would never have two tracks full on one side and no cars on the other side. The danger was that the carferry could actually flip over in its dock and this has happened in real life many times. Little things like this on the model railroad makes for fun operations.

We always called Bill's carferry the *Admiral Dewey*. When I built mine they started calling it the *Commodore Babbish*.

As mentioned, Bill eventually dismantled his model railroad. He had a great big sale of all his rolling stock and buildings one day. He invited a number of his friends over for a final operating session (before he gave me the carferry) and then again for the sale. I purchased from him a number of freight cars, locomotives and buildings. I was able to fill out my railroad very nicely with these.

The buildings really were nice, as many were small background buildings that were not industries receiving freight cars but, instead, stores, gas stations, apartments, etc., that you used for fillers or as scenery in towns. My layout just soaked up all the buildings I purchased and they really added to it. I kept all the business names on them, as many were the names of model railroaders that operated on his layout, some of who come to my layout to operate.

The lower level railroad running on my model railroad thus became the Ann Arbor Railroad traveling from Owosso to Elberta. Operations were usually as follows:

If there were enough operators I assigned a yardmaster to Owosso Yard and Elberta Yard. Their job was to classify arriving trains and make departing trains. The Owosso Yardmaster handled interchanging of cars with GTW and NYC, which come out of a holding track hidden underneath the upper level. Each track had a locomotive and caboose for each interchanging railroad. When the yardmaster had nine or ten cars for one of these two interchanging railroads, he ran the interchanging railroad out of the hidden track into the yard and swapped cars with it from the yard and sent it back to its track. All the cars coming out had been rewaybilled for locations on the railroad other than from where they came. All cars going back were waybilled or were empties for that railroad and would get new destination waybills before they come out again. This spiced up operations a little and not only got more cars on the railroad and provided for a rotation of cars but also got locomotives from different railroads in the scene. AA did interchange with both the NYC and GTW in Owosso.

Also in Owosso, since it was a division point on the railroad and all trains stopped there before being recrewed and cars set off and added onto the train, we had pretend trains coming and going between Owosso and Toledo, Ohio, the southern terminal on the AA. Since the mainline ended at a concrete basement wall in the yard, I accomplished this by using two more hidden holding tracks. Since all trains stopped in Owosso I figured it didn't make any difference if suddenly the train changes direction to head the same geographical direction because it is a new train with a different crew anyway. The yardmaster broke down and classified an arriving train in Owosso and one of the classifications was for cars continuing on the Ann Arbor RR to Toledo.

When nine or ten such cars routed to Toledo were collected, the yardmaster did the same move as it if was an interchange with NYC or GTW: He had an AA train come out of one of the two Toledo holding tracks and swapped its cars with these. The ones coming out were properly waybilled, as were the ones going in and which will be rewaybilled before they come out again. I had an AA locomotive assigned to both of these hidden tracks. Since there were two such Toledo tracks we rotated which one was pulled next, thus not only adding more cars to the railroad but also hiding some for a while.

When the Owosso Yardmaster had trains ready to go, he put road power on them and put them on the departure track in the yard. When a crew was available he assigned them the train and gave them the waybills and permission to depart the yard.

The Elberta yardmaster had a similar job. The difference was that, instead of the Toledo trains or the GTW or NYC interchange, he had the carferry to switch. This got cars out of his yard and new cars into his yard for putting on road trains. In addition to the real carferry, we had a fifteen-car hidden storage yard at the other end of his yard that was leftover from when it was a Soo Line yard. Since AA had two carferry slips in Elberta, we said that this yard was a pretend carferry that was sailing to Wisconsin and we actually routed freight cars to this carferry. This way the only cars going to the real carferry were going to Manistique and cars going to other ports would be routed to the pretend carferry. Again, it got more cars on the railroad and added additional operations to it.

The Elberta Yardmaster also collected cars for the C&O Railroad. The C&O crossed the AA at Thompsonville, between Elberta and Cadillac, and, in reality, interchanged cars there. With some poetic license we said that the C&O came all the way into Elberta Yard to interchange cars and did so from a C&O line behind the mainline that used to be the Soo Line Railroad Eben Junction branch and LS&I interchange on the Soo Line layout. I renamed the partially hidden LS&I yard at the end of the line to be the C&O Boardman Yard in Traverse City and assigned a C&O BL-2 locomotive to it. When Elberta had five C&O cars, I assigned someone to pull five cars from the pickup pocket at Boardman Yard and find the cars in the three-track Boardman Yard, put on a caboose, and run up the branch to Elberta Yard, returning with the cars he picked up there. It was a fun assignment and good for newer operators to get the use to the card system.

The Elberta Yardmaster made up road trains for the eastbound run for Owosso. Most, if not all, road trains from either Elberta or Owosso would have freight cars to set off in Cadillac.

The next major job on the AA was Cadillac Yardmaster. His main responsibility was to switch all the industries in Cadillac. His source of freight cars destined for these industries came from the road trains going through town that set off cars way billed for Cadillac industries. The empties he removed from the industries were then set-off for the road trains to pick up and classified as for either eastbound trains or westbound. He knew what empties to remove from the industries by pulling the cards located behind the pickup divider in the pocket labeled "Cadillac Industries" and finding the freight cars for each card and switching them out of the industry. Likewise, he knew what industries the cars set-off for him by road freights go to by the name of the industry on the waybill.

Usually there were fifteen cars being picked up and fifteen cars being set-off at Cadillac industries each cycle, give or take a few cars. This kept the yardmaster busy. Often, a through-freight appeared in the middle of his work and he had to stop everything and clear out of the way or assist the freight train. He usually made good use of the fact that there was a two-track circle in Cadillac for classifying cars or storing them to get them out of the way. If we had a lot of operators and had doubled-up two of them in Cadillac, a good yardmaster would utilize the fact that he had two local throttles there and would assign his assistant a locomotive and give him power to the inside circle and let him switch the industries off that track (of which most were located, including the elevated industries) while he handled the yard and industries on the outside track.

Cadillac Yardmaster was also responsible for collecting cars that were destined for interchange with the Pennsylvania Railroad. The PRR also had a line through Cadillac and I took advantage of that fact and made the old DSS&A Trout Lake interchange yard into the PRR interchange yard. Like with the C&O interchange, the PRR interchange here (which is physically located right next to the C&O Boardman Yard) had it own locomotive assigned to it and had three tracks. When the Cadillac Yardmaster had five cars in Cadillac Yard for the PRR, I would assign someone to do the pickup pull for the PRR in the hidden yard and then take the PRR train and locomotive to Cadillac to interchange them with the AA there and return with his pickups and put them in the PRR yard. Another short but interesting operation.

In the trackage between Owosso and Cadillac (the longest run on the AA railroad) there was a long passing siding that I called Clare as geographically the city of Clare would be located there on the AA. Much to my surprise, we had very few meets in Clare and the siding rarely got used except sometimes as a long lead track for the yard instead of the Yardmaster using the mainline for this. I guess it was because we had only a few freights running each session and usually Owosso yard, the largest of the freight yards, could handle all trains.

A portion of Clare could not be seen as it ran behind the control panel for the upper level. One day early in the AA era, a freight train came to a dead stop when the locomotives disappeared behind the control panel in Clare. Both of the FA-2s fell to the ground: literally dropped to the floor of the basement. When I investigated to see what caused the derailment by putting my hand back behind the control panel along the tracks I felt something large. I pulled out a naked Barbie doll, obviously placed there by my kids just for this result. We all still talk of the day the naked suicidal Barbie derailed a train in Clare, the worst derailment in the history of the model Ann Arbor Railroad.

One interesting switching operation I created for Cadillac was the routing of freight cars for the Ann Arbor roundhouse there. I used an Atlas turntable, which is rather short and can only handle a single locomotive or one car. Since the turntable had to be moved to line it up for a track alongside the roundhouse where a freight car full of parts or fuel would be spotted, you had no way to move the freight car off the turntable once it was aligned for the correct track as the locomotive would have to be off it due to the lack of room.

Spectrum came out with a model of GE's 44-ton switcher and I bought one. Turns out that the only AA diesel locomotive I did not model was a 44-ton Whitcomb switcher they owned. Since the GE and Whitcomb were very similar in appearance, I decided to paint and decal the GE up as AA #1, their Whitcomb. I put this locomotive on the roundhouse track where the freight cars would be routed and, when there was a delivery to or an empty to leave the roundhouse, we used this engine to move the car on or off the turntable and spot it on the service track, a very short move but, again, an interesting operation. I liked to see if a new Cadillac Yardmaster would figure this move out. Most did not and just left the car on the turntable.

Sometimes we had a lot of cars going either to or from Cadillac. To vary operations, we sometimes moved these cars in a Cadillac Turn train. If they were in Cadillac, we assigned one of both of the RS-1s assigned there to power the train and run it to either Owosso or Elberta Yard and either bring back cars from that yard routed to Cadillac or come back with the light engines and caboose. The same was true with the opposite situation where there was a train of Cadillac cars in Owosso or Elberta. If Cadillac didn't have any pickups for a through train we would run a turn with a light engine out of Cadillac to pick them up.

Cadillac had a shipper, Cadillac Supply Co., that was located east of town off the mainline by the PRR interchange yard. To spice things up we usually required that cars for this shipper be sent out on a local train out of Cadillac complete with a caboose and required the crew to run around their train there before returning so the locomotive was leading and the caboose was at the rear of the train.

CHAPTER 7

MODELING THE GREEN BAY & WESTERN RAILROAD

After operating my model railroads with Ann Arbor RR on the bottom level and my original M&LS on top a couple of years, I started getting in the mood for a change. It is one thing to be in the mood for change and it is another to find the time to make a change on the model railroad. I knew I didn't want to tear anything down and rebuild benchwork or do extensive rewiring. So I started thinking how I could make a radical change to the model railroad yet still keep it simple.

One day the idea occurred to me that the physical layout of the upper level could endear itself to easily become a line of another railroad. There was nothing geographically unique about the upper level. There was no reason it had to be M&LS other than the locations and industries on it were named after M&LS on-line towns and industries. In some ways it was a little odd that I had a rather well known lower level railroad and an obscure upper level railroad.

The really perfect mix of upper and lower railroads from a prototypical perspective with the Ann Arbor RR being on the lower level was to have the upper level being the Green Bay & Western RR in Wisconsin. GBW was a bridge-traffic partner with the Ann Arbor RR and the majority of the carferry interchange across Lake Michigan was with GBW at Kewanee. Everyone who knows about the Ann

Arbor Railroad also knows about GBW and their operational relationship.

Ann Arbor Railroad also ran carferries to the port of Manitowoc, Wisconsin where it interchanged with Chicago Northwestern Railroad and Soo Line Railroad. This too had possibilities, especially since I had already modeled Soo Line and still had plenty of Soo Line freight cars and locomotives. I also liked the CNW and also had plenty of rolling stock for that road too. But I didn't know a lot about the Manitowac operations whereas I did know about the GBW Kewanee to Green Bay, Wisconsin operations. Plus, GBW was a very interesting all-Alco railroad that no one I knew had ever modeled.

The Kewanee to Green Bay portion of GBW was just about as long in real life as the M&LS. It was a rural line that had a few minor towns on-line like M&LS had. Plus, it had two interchanges in Green Bay, one with CNW and one with The Milwaukee Road, just like M&LS had two interchanging railroads at its northern end. Also, Stanley Mailer had just published his epic book on GBW and I had a perfect bible to work from.

The physical fit with GBW was perfect. My M&LS line could easily be changed with very little work to GBW's Kewanee Line. The only problem was that there was very little GBW rolling stock offered by the HO manufacturers and no diesel locomotives painted as such, though all of GBW's locomotive types were represented in HO.

In 1998, I made the decision to change the upper level of the layout to GBW. When I started actually doing it I was amazed at what a perfect fit GBW was.

Here was the project list of things I had to do to convert the upper level to a GBW layout:

- Build new GBW outside-braced boxcars, 50-ton hoppers, and reefers
- Convert M&LS gondolas and flats to GBW ones
- Paint and decal an Alco S-3 for GBW
- Decide what industries for Kewanee
- Build grain elevators for Green Bay and Luxembourg
- Extend run-around/siding at Shingleton
- Build icing platform and lay tracks at the former MP&P site
- Type new waybills for new locations/industries/railroads
- Remove waybills for non-existing industries/locations/railroads
- Revise Car Cards for new railroads/locations/destinations
- Revise control panel schematics for upper level
- Take off 25 to 50 cars?
- Change M&LS caboose to GBW caboose
- New signs for industries

I also prepared a list of issues to contemplate:

- Have C&O carferry track in Kewanee
- How to handle routing for the icing of reefers in Kewanee
- How to handle Anhapee & Western Railroad interchange

- How to handle Milwaukee Road and CNW interchange at Green Bay
- Whether to expand yard in basement workshop
- Industries for the Green Bay sidings
- Track layout in Green Bay (engine house, interchanges?, industries?)

Before I stopped operating the M&LS, I started working on GBW locomotives and rolling stock. You cannot run a railroad without these and I wanted to be pretty close prototypically to what GBW had in the late 1950's. I studied photographs of GBW locomotives and freight cars in the Miller book. GBW had a ton of outside-braced 40-foot wooden boxcars and so I purchased a number of data-only Accurail cars of this type. Though I couldn't find much on other types of GBW freight cars, I assumed that they had some of the standard types of all types of cars of that era and purchased some 55-ton hoppers from Accurail. Champ Decals had come out with GBW decals years ago that I had amassed a number of and I used these to decal up the boxcars and hoppers, coming pretty close to the photographs. It was just my luck that in 1988 Accurail came out with a version of their 40-foot wood reefer factory-painted in a GBW scheme. I purchased a lot of these. I was lucky that Bill had a number of Bev-Bel Athearn 40 foot boxcars painted GBW that I purchased from him when he sold off his railroad and, also at this time, Branchline Trains came out with a 40-foot boxcar painted for GBW. I certainly got lucky with rolling stock, as my timing was perfect for changing over to GBW. Not many prepainted freight cars for GBW existed before this.

I decided to make the cabooses for GBW very simple. I decaled up the M&LS side door caboose for GBW and did the same for two extra cabooses I had purchased from Bill's Erie & Michigan Railroad a couple years back.

Diesels for GBW were another challenge. GBW was an all-Alco railroad. The alleged reason for this was because an important part of their business for many years was shipping wooden car bodies manufactured by Ford Motor Company in their Iron Mountain, Michigan plant, located north of Green Bay in the Upper Peninsula (the wood coming from the Upper Peninsula forests they owned), to the Ford Dearborn River Rouge manufacturing plant outside of Detroit for final assembly. This was why GBW never, and, until the 1960's, the Ann Arbor Railroad also never owned a locomotive made by General Motors (EMD). It was a courtesy to an important shipper: Ford.

In the late 1950s, GBW's locomotive roster consisted of Alco S-1 and S-3 switchers, FA-1 freight power and RS-2/RS-3 and RS-11 roadswitchers. These models were all readily available in plastic in HO Scale at reasonable prices. However, no one at this time had come out with these painted for GBW in their original diesel scheme. In 2000, Walthers did come out with their *Trainline* series of FA-1s in an original GBW paint scheme.

Likewise, no one had come out with decals for an original GBW diesel locomotive paint scheme. This posed a problem that I had to address before I choose modeling GBW. When one looks closely at the GBW paint scheme, it is pretty easy to paint. All it consisted of was a wide gray stripe across a red locomotive ending in a widow's peak on the hoods on a red painted locomotive. The gray stripe was separated from the red by a black line. The GBW rectangle logo "Green Bay Route" appeared on the ends of the locomotive (in black) and below the window on the cab of the switchers and roadswitchers (in red). Microscale had a GBW modern boxcar decal sheet that included the red logo that I needed. Champ Decal's discontinued road name series decal set for GBW included the black logo that was still fairly available at hobby stores.

What I did was paint up an Atlas S-3 switcher, an Atlas RS-3 and RS-11 roadswitcher and two E-R Import Brazilian-made FA-1s in the GBW paint scheme. This was enough power for me to run my upper level. I used the two FA-1s on the Green Bay to Kewanee freights, the RS-11 to switch Norwood Yard in Green Bay, and the S-2 and RS-3 were assigned to Kewanee.

I painted each shell red then masked off the large stripe and painted it gray using Floquil's Caboose Red and Reefer Gray. Then I used Champ's black stripe decals and ran them along the gray stripe border on the top and bottom (this helped cover any rough lines between the two colors). Next I used the red Microscale GBW logo decal on the roadswitcher and switcher cabs below the window in the gray area and the gray Champ logo decal at the ends of the long and short hood for the roadswitchers and at the end of the long hood for the switcher. For the FA-1s I put the red logo decal at the front of the locomotive in the gray band.

I had to come up with some new, appropriate industries for GBW. This was easy in Green Bay on the layout as there was a large grain elevator located in Norwood Yard and the paper industry was an important customer in Green Bay on the north side of town. Good old Walthers' Cornerstone Series came out with a nice grain elevator about this time. I bought it and built it as a flat, cutting the elevator in half and laying one half along the wall in Norwood Yard at the end of a long siding I had there. I used the other half as the major industry in Luxembourg Siding, the former Stueben Siding on M&LS, as in real life this was the location of a large Cargill elevator that was the main reason GBW built it's Kewanee, Green Bay & Western subsidiary line from Green Bay to Kewanee. I kept the existing M&LS/DSS&A industries in Green Bay as they were generic enough and changed the pulpwood siding into a storage track for the road locomotives. At the old LS&I siding in Green Bay in the railroad room I made a flat of the Cornerstone Furniture Company and named it Fort Howard Paper. This had the double stub-end track going to it, giving it plenty of room to set off cars for this important industry.

Also in Green Bay, on the side in the railroad room, I extended the run around there so it could accommodate a twelve-car train. This track then became the arrival departure yard for Norwood Yard, relieving a lot of congestion in the other room and in the freight yard

located there. When the Norwood switcher made up a

Kewanee Turn he set off the completed train on this departure track in the other room (a fun move in itself), freeing up some yard space in Norwood, then pulled the cars from the arriving turn that were left on the other, arrival, track. The crews of the turn then brought the power from Norwood yard to this track and coupled onto the train.

Norwood yard consisted of the six ex-DSS&A and LS&I interchange tracks in the other room. The way it worked was that there was a set-off, hold and pickup box for Norwood Yard's cards. New trains are made up based on what cards were in the pickup box. Arriving trains were carded in the set-off box. As a new train leaves, the cards in the set-off box rotated to the hold box and the cards in the hold box become pickup cards for the next train. This kept the yard full and it took three cycles before a car left Norwood Yard and went back on the layout in a train. The Norwood Elevator had its own siding and the other long industrial siding in Green Bay had four industries on it. As cars arrived from Kewanee for these industries, the Norwood switcher cut them out and switched these industries and Fort Howard Paper on the other side of the wall as a separate switch job, using a caboose. This created some interesting switching here as you had industries located in two rooms and only a small five-car run-around track to work with. Whoever was assigned Norwood Yard usually had a very busy and fun night. Since the crew in Norwood Yard was never interfered with by through trains and could pretty much operate at their own pace, I used this job as a training ground for future yardmasters and switch crews as it gave the crew a relaxed atmosphere to figure out the card system and the geography of the layout.

The usual drill was that there was a freight train originating out of Norwood Yard in Green Bay for Kewanee every session. A crew was assigned this train, which was already made up and was on the departure track in Green Bay. The FA-1s were the assigned power though I had bought a pair of Baldwin Sharks in the demonstrator paint scheme to supplement the FA's, saying GBW was trying them out and thinking of buying them from Baldwin. This gave the road crews some variety in road locomotives and the Sharks sure looked great on the layout. This train worked Luxembourg Siding and Casco Junction on its run to Kewanee. Casco Junction was a siding that was used as an interchange track with the Anhapee & Western RR. When arriving at Kewanee, he got the Kewanee Yardmaster's permission to come into the yard. The Yardmaster directed the Kewanee Turn to set off its train and usually had a twelve-car train for it to take back to Green Bay. On the way back it switched Clyde Siding (the old Hiawatha Siding) and Luxembourg Siding again, if needed. When it arrived in the arrival track in Green Bay the train was done and the crew went onto other jobs.

The Anhapee & Western Railroad existed on my model railroad. It was at the old down ramp switchback that once connected the two levels. In the level between the upper and lower level where the switchback was there were two tracks there that was Sturgeon, Wisconsin at the northern terminal of A&W. A&W had two GE 70-tonners as power after they retired steam, both in a Southern Pacific-type orange and black scheme. I purchased two Bachman Spectrum series 70-tonners in the SP scheme, painted out the words Southern Pacific on the hood, and used these coupled together for the A&W trains. They had a very steep grade up to Casco Junction which they could only make with one or two cars and it caused all sorts of excitement during an operating session when they stalled on the hill or, worse yet, lost a car on the hill that rolled all the way back down to Sturgeon. The A&W was a fun little operation on the layout.

With the changeover to GBW, the City of Manistique, Michigan became the City of Kewanee, Wisconsin. The major change to this town was the converting old Manistique Pulp & Paper Company to Kewanee Shipbuilding Company. Merely changing the name easily did this. Since Kewanee was the end of the line before a long carferry trip and a lot of perishables were travelling cross-country on this route, I needed a refrigerator car icing platform in Kewanee. I purchased the icing platform that Walthers' Cornerstone Series had just come out with. It fit well where one of the two of the pulpwood tracks and the MP&P locomotive servicing track were with the shorter siding being for arriving ice in refrigerator cars and the longer siding being where the loaded refrigerator cars were iced before sailing across Lake Michigan or after arriving in Kewanee. The Kewanee Yardmaster had orders to ice all loaded reefers coming or going via the carferry.

All the other industries in Kewanee retained their old M&LS Manistique names, which made the transition easy. The only other thing I did was build a four-track stub-end yard at the end of Kewanee over Owosso Yard on the lower level. The purpose of this yard was to make it a pretend C&O carferry as the C&O also sailed to Kewanee. This way I could route cars to the C&O ferry and, after the Kewanee Yardmaster had accumulated ten or twelve of them, he could pull one of the four tracks there (pretending it was an arriving C&O carferry by pulling the track that had the waybills ready for pickup) and then put the cars he collected into that track (loading the C&O carferry). He then rotated the cards so that this track would be the last to be picked up in the cycle. This way we got thirty some extra cars on the layout out of this new extension. Also, with the C&O interchange on the lower level, it made no difference if a car was waybilled to go to the C&O on either level, as there was a C&O interchange on both railroads.

The Kewanee Yardmaster was kept very busy and, if we had extra people at an operating session, I often assigned him a helper. Because of this, I assigned two GBW diesels to Kewanee, the S-3 and the RS-3, so both people could be operating a locomotive.

Of course, changing the upper level to GBW required a large rewrite of the waybills and car cards. Not only did we have a new railroad but we also had new cities and sidings and new industries. Even if the industry name remained unchanged on a waybill the name of the railroad and the city it was located in had to change. The "empty, return to" information on many of the cards had to be changed from M&LS to GBW. And, in addition to the somewhat simplistic though large task of doing this clerical work, was the more important task of making sure enough cars were routed to these new locations and how this would affect the flow of freight cars on both levels.

I cheated a little this time in that I did not retype all new waybills or car cards for these changes as I had done in the past but, instead, typed out labels that I could then stick to the waybills and car cards to cover up the old writings and show the new information. I also used the computer to print out these labels instead of sticking the waybill or car card into the manual typewriter as I had in the past. I also had to remove waybills to non-existent locations and industries and add some new waybills for new places. Though this seemed like it would be an overwhelming job, it really wasn't that bad. It was the type of job that I could take to my office and do a little at a time during lunchtimes and pretty much get the job done in a few weeks.

The big day came when I had my first operating session with the upper level being GBW, which was in early 1999. I had told no one about the transition and everyone was surprised when they arrived for that first session. Some expressed disappointment as they liked M&LS and thought it was a quaint railroad to model. Others loved the idea of GBW as it made more sense in the scheme of Ann Arbor RR and was a railroad they knew something about and could relate to more. For me it was a way to have some fun doing some new model railroad building and planning without making major structural changes and without costing a lot of money or taking my model railroad out of operation for any large amount of time. I too missed M&LS as it was my first model railroad and I always thought it was a great railroad to model. But I really got into GBW and had no regrets about modeling it.

CHAPTER 8

MODELING THE GRAND TRUNK WESTERN AND CANADIAN NATIONAL RAILROADS

On September 4, 2003 I had my last operating session on my model railroad of the Ann Arbor Railroad and the Green Bay and Western Railroad. It was an impromptu last session organized just a couple of days beforehand. I had four friends over at the last session and, since I didn't let it out that it was to be the last one, it went just as a normal operating session did. We had a lot of fun and moved a lot of cars. I took a lot of photographs and also videotaped the session, which was a little suspicious to them. I let the session linger on about an hour longer than usual, as no one seemed in any hurry to leave. Everyone eventually finished up their jobs and then went home.

About a year beforehand I decided to pursue my dream of having a layout of Grand Trunk Western Railroad. I came up with a very good concept of how to do so using my present benchwork and most of the trackwork.

My plans for the lower level of the layout were to make a shift from modeling a large geographic area (Owosso to Frankfurt) covering over a hundred real miles to one covering only five miles. Same for the upper level: going from 50 miles to about three miles. I also planned on shifting from operating road trains that ran between cities to a terminal urban operation on both levels.

My lower level became the Grand Trunk Western

Dequindre Line of its Holly Subdivision between the Detroit River and East Yard in Detroit. My upper level became Canada National Railways' Windsor, Ontario operations. The two levels are connected with the Detroit River Carferry operations of CN and GTW. The era is the late 1950's.

Both these geographic locations were very heavily industrialized and kept both railroads very busy with round-the-clock switching of the many industries located on these lines. Both lines had passenger operations. A carferry operation across the Detroit River was the interchange between the two railroads. CN owned GTW so there was a lot of both railroads' freight cars on both railroads. Steam locomotives in the form of road power, passenger power and switchers still ran on both lines up until 1960.

I had always wanted to model GTW and being able to do it and including a CN layout too was a perfect fit for my two-level layout. I had been collecting plenty of GTW and CN locomotives (steam and diesel) and rolling stock. I kept my present benchwork and just revised some trackage to switch it over. I loved switching anyway and doing a model of a five-mile industrial line meant a lot of switching. I was able to keep the carferry operations. I added passenger trains and steam locomotives. And best of all, I had very little benchwork and trackwork changes to do for this change.

Of course, everything changed from that point on. I needed a ton of new buildings built for the new industries. All my "Northern Michigan" backdrop scenes had to become urban scenes. My card system needed to be redone from scratch for all the new locations and industries and new rolling stock being added.

I took off most of my Ann Arbor and GBW rolling stock and locomotives and sold them. Many of the rural buildings, like grain elevators, had to come off. I had to completely redo what was the City of Cadillac in the center of the lower level and that was where most of my track changes and benchwork changes occurred. I decided to continue to use my Lake Michigan carferries as Detroit River carferries even though they were completely different in design.

Instead of recollecting and writing about my Grand Trunk Western/Canadian National model railroad from scratch, I will reproduce an article I wrote about it for the Grand Trunk Western Historical Society newsletter "*Semaphore*" a few years ago in its entirety, adding to it some photographs of this layout.

Modeling GTW's "Dinky Line" in HO Scale

Grand Trunk Western's Dequindre Line, affectionately known as the "Dinky Line," offers model railroaders a very interesting prototype railroad for modeling that combines heavy industry switching with through-freight and passenger operations.

The four miles of the Dinky Line that ran from the Detroit River to Milwaukee Junction was probably the most industry-dense portion of the entire GTW system up to the late 1970's. After that point, industries located on this line and the amount of shipping by railroad by the remaining industries dropped off dramatically. Going back to the 1940's through the 1960's, GTW required crews 24-hours a day to keep the customers happy on this short stretch of track. Add to this the intercity passenger trains (until 1971) and the commuter trains (up to 1983) that traversed this line, plus the freight inter-yard transfers and the carferry operations occurring at the same time, and it was one busy stretch of track. No wonder it was four tracks wide most of these four miles.

What this provides the modeler is either a very compact model railroad that can fit into a small physical space or the opportunity to have a very detailed and busy operating railroad in a larger physical space. Either way, the Dinky Line is a dream come true for the GTW modeler that likes a switching/operation type of model railroad.

What makes the Dinky Line unique is that it is not all located on a flat, uninteresting terrain. There is a 90-degree bend of the line when it reaches the Detroit River and enters Boat Yard, City Yard and Brush Street Station. The two miles between this bend and north of Gratiot Avenue is all below grade with the many city streets passing over the track on bridges and with the loading docks on the industries in Eastern Market located below street level, a unique modeling possibility.

There were many yards and team tracks that all were on curves or angles due to the lack of physical space. The industries served on this line were very diverse including automotive, food storage, meat packers, building materials, cement/grain/flour elevators and heavy industry. The buildings they used are all of a classic early 20th Century style that are fun to model and can be duplicated with the many available HO scale kits offered.

The passenger operations are fun to model, not only at Brush Street Station at the end of the line but also the constant parade of passenger trains traversing the line that the switching crews had to get out of the way of. An interesting point is that until March 27, 1960 GTW used steam engines on all their passenger and commuter trains on this line and did light engine moves after each train to service and turn the locomotives at its Milwaukee Junction engine house located at the north end of the Dinky Line. You could keep one operator busy just running passenger trains and running its locomotives back and forth at an operating session. GTW continued this practice into the 1960's with its diesel passenger power before just running them in reverse on the next train out of town.

You could also include Milwaukee Junction engine facilities on the model railroad of this line as it was at the northern end and had a direct access track to this line. Here GTW serviced all its Detroit locomotive fleet, not only the locomotives servicing the Dinky Line.

The carferry operations across the Detroit River to parent Canadian National allow for a very interesting model railroad operation. The famous *Lansdowne* side-wheeler was the main carferry used by GTW here.

Depending on your interests or physical limitations, not all aspects of the Dinky Line would have to be modeled. If you are only interested in industrial switching, you can just do that and forego the passenger and carferry operations. If you prefer the passenger and carferry operations you could just model the riverfront aspects of the line. Not enough room for four tracks? Model just one or two tracks.

Do you like the steam era? GTW used steam on this line very late in both the form of passenger locomotives and switchers. Do you like the diesel era? GTW used EMD and Alco switchers on this line as well as GP-9s on interyard transfers and even their two Alco RS-1s from time to time. Like the present era? The line is now owned by the Detroit Connecting Railroad using an EMD and GE switcher and interchanging with GTW at East Yard in Detroit.

I went from modeling in HO scale the Ann Arbor Railroad from Owosso to Frankfort (100 plus miles) to the four-mile Dequindre Line using the same amount of space and bench work. The modeling of such a small segment of track opened up so many possibilities I hadn't imagined before. Of course, it helped that I prefer an operations railroad to one where I am just running through-freights.

Even so, I had to make a lot of compromises on my Dinky Line. Mine is a two-track line, basically half the real Dinky Line. The real Dinky Line's two-track mainline and two outside industrial tracks were more than I had room for or that I would ever use. So I have a one-track mainline with one industrial track the length of the railroad with plenty of crossovers. Whenever a passenger train comes through the local switching crew still has to get their cars off the mainline to clear.

Though my bench work is flat, I created the illusion of the below-grade portion of the Dinky Line by having many overpasses crossing the track at my Eastern Market area and the loading docks on the buildings there thus appearing to be below grade.

I did not have room for an actual Brush Street Station so I just have two tracks alongside the City/Boat Yard for use by the passenger trains. The yard engine assigned to this yard also services the passenger trains. The Robin Hood Flour industry that was located on the Detroit River there is a three-track yard without a building and is not physically located next to Brush Street Station as it was in real life due to physical limitations. Most of the riverfront industries served by GTW on my layout are sidings with either flats or even no buildings for the same reasons. I took photographs of some of the buildings on the Dinky Line and had them blown up in size and use them as backdrops in the Detroit River area on my layout instead of model buildings due to space limitations.

I model in 1958 and so have a mixture of steam and diesels on my Dinky Line. I do have an East Yard where most of the cars for the line are generated by GTW through-freights and New York Central, Detroit Toledo Shore Line and Detroit Terminal Railroad interchanges that are in a hidden storage yard. I have an East Yard Yardmaster assignment at one end of the layout that also handles the above-mentioned interchanges, a City Yard/Boat Yard assignment at the other end that also handles Brush Street Station and the carferry, a Dequindre Line crew and a City Job crew at my operating sessions.

My layout covers three walls in my basement and includes a large peninsula in the middle. The peninsula is the Dinky Line industrial area with the two outside wall ends of the layout forming the ends of the "U" being East Yard and City/Boat Yard and the shorter wall being the industrial trackage along the Detroit River. Not all of the peninsula is trackage and industries. Across the center of it is Dequindre Avenue, the street that parallels the Dinky Line, and on Dequindre Avenue are various shops and businesses that have no railroad connection. This gives the overall impression of an urban setting.

I do not have a Milwaukee Junction engine house. Though I do have some passenger steam locomotives for the passenger/commuter trains, I do not turn them but, instead, run them without a train to the opposite point of the railroad where they take the next passenger train, thus each engine is always taking a passenger train the same direction for convenience. Even though GTW stopped using their "doodlebug" gas electric by this time on the Mount Clemens Subdivisions, I do operate one out of Brush Street Station just to add a little variety to the passenger operations (and one more passenger train to get in the way of the switching crews!).

I have two carferries that we load freight cars onto and sail across the Detroit River. My layout has two levels. The Dinky Line is the lower and much larger layout. Above this level along the three walls and into an adjoining room is Windsor, Ontario and the Canadian National Railway operations located on that side of the Detroit River.

Like GTW's Dequindre Line, the upper level CN Windsor terminal operations is compressed and compact. Not only does it give me an excuse for modeling CN, but also it gives me a place for the carferries to sail to and actually load and unload freight cars. Though much smaller in size and operation than the Dinky Line, I nevertheless assign an operator to Windsor to handle the carferry and industrial switching there and also assign an operator at nearby Walkerville Yard where interchange is made with the Canadian Pacific Railway and shortline Essex Terminal Railroad. There are also some industries, like Hiram Walker distillers and Chrysler's Windsor assembly plant, located in Walkerville, the name of an area on the east side of The City of Windsor and switched by CN.

CN freights from Toronto arrive at the Boat Yard in Windsor with cars for the carferry and local industries. CN freights for Toronto leave the boat yard with all CN-waybilled cars. Walkerville Yard, located in the other room of the basement, is where these trains originate and end due to space limitations.

CN also ran passenger trains between Windsor and Toronto and I have one on my layout. We run this passenger train into Brush Street Station across the river in Detroit via the carferry after it arrives in Windsor, just like CN did at one time with one of its Toronto/Windsor passenger trains.

As in real life, it was never CN that was the big operator of trains in Windsor but, instead, the Wabash Railroad. Wabash had trackage rights over CN to Fort Erie/Buffalo. It connected with this track in Windsor via its own carferries from Detroit at one time.

So, to be prototypical, I have a Wabash switcher assigned to Windsor Boat Yard and a pair of Wabash F-7A's that I use for the Wabash freight trains running out of and into Windsor over CN. The Wabash carferry is made up of just staging tracks instead of a real carferry. All cars entering the upper level eventually end up on the Wabash staging tracks via a Wabash train to get them out of rotation for a while and rewaybilled. Like the CN freight trains, the Wabash freights originate or terminate at Walkerville Yard in the other room simulating run-throughs to and from Fort Erie, New York due to space limitations.

Local industries are serviced out of either Windsor Yard

or Walkerville Yard by CN crews. CP and Essex Terminal trains come into Walkerville yard to interchange and the C&O Canada Lines interchange is out of Windsor Yard with C&O power coming out of a staging area to do the interchange.

Both my Dinky Line lower level layout and my CN Windsor terminal line upper level of my layout can be run independent of one another or together. The Windsor portion of the layout adds a lot of depth to the Dinky Line, as it gives a real place for freight cars to go when switched onto the Detroit River carferries at the Boat Yard in Detroit.

My steam engines are mostly brass CN and GTW models that I have collected over the years. My diesels are a mixture of all current and older model plastic models with the majority being Proto 1000/2000 models. Some are decaled by me using the many GTW and CN decals available. My freight cars try to model the types of cars and railroads that came onto the Dinky Line in 1958. There are a lot of refrigerator cars due to the packing companies and cold storage plants located online. There are lot of covered hoppers due to the cement and grain elevators located online. All are commercially available kits that I have been collecting over the years and many are lettered for GTW. Some were undecorated cars decaled appropriately.

I use a basic electrical system utilizing electrical blocks instead of a command control system; though a command control system would probably work well with all the switching and through-train activities on the layout. There is a control panel for both levels with a track layout schematic and six-position rotaries for the blocks. Throttles are color-coded and four can be used on both levels with one each unique to each level. Tethered throttles are used for the yards and walk-around throttles for road and switching trains.

I have been real pleased with my Dinky Line model railroad. This is the fourth model railroad I have had and is the first industrial-setting one and covers the shortest physical distance in real life of any of the others. I can keep four or five operators very busy during an operating session and can accommodate a couple more operators comfortably on it, if needed. What makes it especially fun is trying to operate it as close as possible to how the real life Dinky Line was run based on the information provided me by retired GTW employees who once worked on it and also from my own observations of this line.

As of writing this book, the GTW/CN layout is still in operation. I have made some minor changes to it, such as adding some locomotives and removing others. I try to have operating sessions once every couple months, usually with just a couple other operators. I have had as many as six operators over at one time and the railroad ran well.

With this, the story of my ever-changing model railroad adventure ends, for now. Now you understand my Model Train Madness. It is an incurable disease that just mutates into new phases as time goes by.

ABOUT THE AUTHOR

Byron Babbish is a railroad photographer, writer, and historian. A retired attorney, his time is now devoted to teaching law, model railroading, playing violin and writing.

Printed in Great Britain
by Amazon.co.uk, Ltd.,
Marston Gate.